First World War
and Army of Occupation
War Diary
France, Belgium and Germany

59 DIVISION
177 Infantry Brigade,
Brigade Machine Gun Company
23 February 1917 - 28 February 1918

WO95/3023/7

The Naval & Military Press Ltd
www.nmarchive.com
Published in association with The National Archives

Published by

The Naval & Military Press Ltd

Unit 10 Ridgewood Industrial Park,

Uckfield, East Sussex,

TN22 5QE England

Tel: +44 (0) 1825 749494

www.naval-military-press.com

www.nmarchive.com

This diary has been reprinted in facsimile from the original. Any imperfections are inevitably reproduced and the quality may fall short of modern type and cartographic standards.

© Crown Copyright
Images reproduced by permission of The National Archives, London, England, 2015.

Contents

Document type	Place/Title	Date From	Date To
Heading	WO95/3023/8 Brigade Machine Gun Company		
Heading	59th Division 177th Infy Bde 177th Machine Gun Coy. Feb 1917-Apr 1918		
War Diary	Havre	23/02/1917	23/02/1917
War Diary	Longeast	24/02/1917	25/02/1917
War Diary	Bayonvillers	25/02/1917	06/03/1917
War Diary	Foucaucourt	07/03/1917	08/03/1917
War Diary	Trenches	09/03/1917	20/03/1917
War Diary	Foucaucourt	21/03/1917	26/03/1917
War Diary	Eterpigny	27/03/1917	27/03/1917
War Diary	Leohesiel	28/03/1917	28/03/1917
War Diary	Hancourt	29/03/1917	02/04/1917
War Diary	Raisel	03/04/1917	20/04/1917
War Diary	Bernes	21/04/1917	29/04/1917
War Diary	Jeancourt	30/04/1917	15/05/1917
War Diary	Vraignes	16/05/1917	26/05/1917
War Diary	Equancourt	27/05/1917	27/05/1917
War Diary	Dessart Wood	28/05/1917	31/05/1917
War Diary	Gouzeaucourt Wood	01/06/1917	22/06/1917
War Diary	Equancourt	23/06/1917	01/07/1917
War Diary	V 6.a.0.9	02/07/1917	31/07/1917
Operation(al) Order(s)	Operation Order No 1 by Capt G.R. King Comndg 177th Machine Gun Coy	23/07/1917	23/07/1917
Operation(al) Order(s)	Operation Order No 2 by Capt G.R. King Comndg 177th Machine Gun Coy	26/07/1917	26/07/1917
War Diary	O16.a.09	01/08/1917	22/08/1917
War Diary	Serlis	23/08/1917	30/08/1917
War Diary	Albert	31/08/1917	31/08/1917
Operation(al) Order(s)	Operation Order No 3 by Capt G.R. King Comndg 177th Machine Gun Coy	11/08/1917	11/08/1917
War Diary	J9d.1.8 Sheet 27 Belgium	01/09/1917	20/09/1917
War Diary	L 15.b.9.1	21/09/1917	23/09/1917
War Diary	Goldfish Chateau	24/09/1917	24/09/1917
War Diary	Trenches	25/09/1917	30/09/1917
Miscellaneous	Appendix To War Diary For Month Of September 1917		
War Diary	G 5.e.6.4 Map Belg 28SW	01/10/1917	02/10/1917
War Diary	St. Venant	03/10/1917	06/10/1917
War Diary	Erny St Julien	07/10/1917	10/10/1917
War Diary	Bours	11/10/1917	11/10/1917
War Diary	Maisnelles Ruitz	12/10/1917	12/10/1917
War Diary	Carency	13/10/1917	14/10/1917
War Diary	Trenches	15/10/1917	22/10/1917
War Diary	Carency	23/10/1917	31/10/1917
Operation(al) Order(s)	177th Machine Gun Company Operation Order No. 8	20/10/1917	20/10/1917
Operation(al) Order(s)	Operation Order No 6 by Capt G.R. King Comndg 177th Machine Gun Coy		
War Diary	Carency	01/11/1917	06/11/1917
War Diary	Lievin	07/11/1917	16/11/1917
War Diary	Carency	17/11/1917	19/11/1917
War Diary	Bellacourt	20/11/1917	22/11/1917

War Diary	Achiete Le Petit	23/11/1917	23/11/1917
War Diary	Dessart Wood	24/11/1917	27/11/1917
War Diary	Trescault	28/11/1917	28/11/1917
War Diary	Flesquieres	29/11/1917	30/11/1917
Miscellaneous	Operation Order By Capt. G.R King Commanding 177th Machine Gun Coy	05/11/1917	05/11/1917
War Diary	Flesquieres	01/12/1917	08/12/1917
War Diary	Frescault	09/12/1917	17/12/1917
War Diary	Flesquires	18/12/1917	23/12/1917
War Diary	Bertincourt	24/12/1917	24/12/1917
War Diary	Rocquigny	25/12/1917	25/12/1917
War Diary	Lignereuil	26/12/1917	31/01/1918
War Diary	Penin	01/02/1918	12/02/1918
War Diary	Trenches	13/02/1918	26/02/1918
War Diary	In Field	27/02/1918	28/02/1918

WO95/3023/8

Brigade Machine Gun
Company

59TH DIVISION
177TH INFY BDE

177TH MACHINE GUN COY.

FEB 1 917-APR 1918

Army Form C. 2118.

SECRET

WAR DIARY
or
INTELLIGENCE SUMMARY

177 Company Machine Gun Corps

February 1917   Vol 1

(Erase heading not required.)

Instructions regarding War Diaries and Intelligence Summaries are contained in F. S. Regs., Part II. and the Staff Manual respectively. Title Pages will be prepared in manuscript.

Place	Date	Hour	Summary of Events and Information	Remarks and references to Appendices
Havre	23/2/17	9- am	The 177 Coy M.G.C. arrived in France disembarked at Lehavre.	
"	"	3.30	The Company entrained for Longpres.	
Longpres	24/2/17	6 am	The Company arrived at Longpres.	
"	25/2/17	9.30 am	" left for Bayonvillers	
Bayonvillers	25/2/17	3 pm	" arrived at Bayonvillers were billeted	
"	26/2/17		Company billeted at Bayonvillers.	
"	27/2/17	9 am	C.O. left for a tour of the trenches to be taken over by the 177 Coy	
"	28/2/17		Company at Bayonvillers.	
Bayonvillers	1/3/17		"	
	2		"	
	3		"	
	4		"	
	5		"	

for O.C. No. 177 M.G. Coy.

ORDERLY ROOM
Date 9.3.17
177 M.G. COMPANY

WAR DIARY

INTELLIGENCE SUMMARY

177 Coy M.G.C.
original
Vol II

MARCH 1917

Army Form C. 2118.
SECRET

Place	Date	Hour	Summary of Events and Information	Remarks and references to Appendices
Bayonvillers	1/3/17		Company Paraded as per Coy. order. Weekly clean small arms.	Weekly
"	2/3/17		Company paraded at 9-0 a.m. supplied with 35 maps, received clean vermorals from Brigade H.Q.	Weekly arm.
"	3/3/17		Company paraded at 9-0 am as per order.	As arm.
"	4/3/17		Company paraded as per orders. Lieut. Wilhot left for the trenches. 150 Brigade H.Q. The guns (16 Vickers) were tested in a quarry at Vermorand map Ref ROSIERES combined sheet 1:40,000 V18 a 70.50 or Amiens 17 1:100,000 road going SW of Vermorand. All guns recorded well. Fired 250 rounds per gun, numbers 1 & 2 firing. The men were given Bore Designation steel + No 1 & 2 R.T. + Sedols revolver forester Barrel cases were filled with oakum & glycerine. Weather fine, drizzle by midday, SE wind.	

Army Form C. 2118.

WAR DIARY
or
INTELLIGENCE SUMMARY
(Erase heading not required.)

Army ??????

Place	Date	Hour	Summary of Events and Information	Remarks and references to Appendices
Bayonvillers	4/3/17		Coy A. Received two extra maps for Brigade HQ Sheet Road 53903 attacked Hospital and camps — contact with Pte Read 43630 were discharged medically fit	1,2,3,4,5,6,7
"	5/3/17		Heavy fall of snow during the night (King) took over duties of Lieut Renton. General clean up. Returns of supplies for Rehols 184 (including 52 deposited hospital camp high) did company went domestic billets at a.m. on billets. 2/Lieut Raymond L. Anderson SA + Towner w/ left for the trenches in town of inspection	??????
"	6/3/17		Company left Bayonvillers at 12 noon for Toutencourt weather fold N.E. wind Arrived at Buature Camp at 3.30 pm. Billeted at Nutents. The accommodation was had no arrangements for men.	??????
Toutencourt	7/3/17		Company billeted in huts at Buature Camp Toutencourt Section 243 left for Greebr at 9.15 pm to relieve respective Section of the 150th RE Company	??????

WAR DIARY or INTELLIGENCE SUMMARY

Army Form C. 2118.

original

Place	Date	Hour	Summary of Events and Information	Remarks and references to Appendices
Foucaucourt	7/3/17		Contd. Weather very cold throughout N.E. wind. The relief was carried out very satisfactorily. Drew 100 pair Gum boots thigh at Foucaucourt.	
	8/3/17		Section H.Q. moved into the line leaving limbers camp at 5.45 p.m. The relief was completed at 9.30 p.m. Ranges satisfactorily. Enemy M.G. opened fire in reply at 7.30 p.m. Weather very cold today. N.E. wind strong, changing to N.W. about 4.30 p.m.	6.37 a.m.
Gueches	9/3/17		Capt. Suffield, Lieut. Willett wanted No 2 dugout H.Q. return M.G. emplacements, alternative positions communications. Two of No 2 Lickers' guns are actually in emplacements, positions were accidentally shifted to cover H.Ms. The targets although very shallow were plainly being frozen. Enemy T.Ms. were fairly general over the area protected by H1 company H.G. There was a slow fall of snow (2 ins). Wind N.E. to S.E. with breeze. Trenches in a bad muddy state. Hen stewful	WX GWP

WAR DIARY / INTELLIGENCE SUMMARY

Army Form C. 2118

Place	Date	Hour	Summary of Events and Information	Remarks and references to Appendices
Tendres	10/3/17	4.30 am	Capt. Sheffield & Lieut. Willett visited No. 3 Section the front H.Q. Emplacements are very unsatisfactory & alternative positions were shot. No. 2 – as only possible to work during the night at the trenches are in such a bad condition that it is impossible to complete. Alterations to gun positions were done, the guns referred to have been repaired. No. 1 Section guns were firing during the night on enemy positions.	
Tendres	11/3/17		A misty day with sunshine, Capt. Sheffield visited Brigade H.Q. There was considerable artillery activity on both sides, the enemy in particular shelling Battery Road. No. 4 Section Ration party lost their way in the fog & part of it officers Lt. K. N.777 h.L.Cpy were buried in a fall of a dug out. There were other casualties.	W.S. Ax
Tendres	12/3/17		The morning the rays of direction boards to trenches is invaluable especially in the difficulty felt by men not accustomed in the system of trenches, last night in trying to find way to the system might with advantage be extended out for the benefit of wandering patrols. The H.Q. details assisted in the repair of trenches.	W.S. Cort

WAR DIARY / INTELLIGENCE SUMMARY

Army Form C. 2118.

Place	Date	Hour	Summary of Events and Information	Remarks and references to Appendices
Trenches	13/3/17		Meteorological - Rain - Cleared snow. Trenches falling in from the thaw. Ration parties had great difficulty in reaching the guns at night. Guns did not fire owing to infantry Relief taking place. O/C 175th H.g.C. army arrived to arrange to relieve 177 bny. Lieut Pinkett 2nd in command of 177 H.g.C. also arrived. The wire Capt Oldfield Lt. H.E. Lee from A.D.S. removed to hospital by ambulance owing to illness.	178 am
	14/3/17		Major Puckle 4 Officers of 175 H.g. Coy & 47 NCOs & men came as advance party for mortisters, prior to taking over relief of 177 bny. The party went over their respective gun positions generally informed of the situation therein. The normal guns were fired.	4/3 Corps
	15/3/17		Weather fine. Some enemy shelling along the L.H. intermediate line, otherwise a quiet day. The trench companies complained of the bad condition of the between road. His divisional carrier catered a board of enquiry at Stonewood. 9 horses of the company were accidentally killed owing to the collapse of their dugout roof owing to the expenditure of their stables by the public.	

WAR DIARY
INTELLIGENCE SUMMARY
(Erase heading not required.)

Army Form C. 2118.

Place	Date	Hour	Summary of Events and Information	Remarks and references to Appendices
Trescles	15/3/17		Contd:- A new alternative position forward explored to No. 14 position was today completed. The enemy in his retreat has so far suffered no casualties though only slight access to battlefield.	N.S. con
	16/3/17		During the early morning later from Brig. Gen. Jones C/S Brig. 21st Division b.13 visited old dugouts at 9.11am. Capt. Duffield visited the Brigade HQ. Artillery on both enemy's & our own were quiet. 177 Company relief carried out officers of 175 company returned to their H.Q. Sunshine all day.	605 con
	17/3/17	6-0	Our artillery putting a barrage over the Euenstown in the early morning. We fired approx seventy five [a] 7.0 rounds [?] each gun & burst B. 7. 8. 9. 9½. During the morning the Infantry (Leicesters) advanced by Boatham [?] found the trenches evacuated, the enemy having retired across the Somme. The Battalion 3/4 moved their guns into new position forward in the direction of Gricourt Wood. The O.C. reconnoitred for new Bty gun position. The company went in reserve to move on Bn position. Section 34th Company atd [?] O.P. HQ (D.C. Beaufort [?]) An officer from each section att set [?]	M.Sel.M

WAR DIARY or INTELLIGENCE SUMMARY

Army Form C. 2118.

Place	Date	Hour	Summary of Events and Information	Remarks and references to Appendices
Trenches	19/3/17		Eveline all day. Everything quiet. Sporting burey repairing roads.	
			A strong party of the enemy were seen permanently attached to 177th Coy in left Brigade as a carrying party, reported at 10.30 pm.	
			The force reconnoitering as far as the Somme was small enemy patrol on the opposite side of the Canal.	
	19/3/17		Fine weather. The left wing R.F.A. took possession over H.Q. on Brigade authority & still moved forward to new H.Q. at Hitler Buildings in the German supports.	LDS 411
			The condition of the enemy trenches wagon & within went substantial dugout and huts drown by enemy to as to be useless to us.	
			No. 177 Company found H.Q. at N.36.0.1.2.	
			A carrying party attached to No 3 section consisted of 2 men of the section & 60 of the 5th Lincoln were engaged the old German position when 1 bomb was accidentally killed 1 Pte of the men engaged, 3 seriously among the latter were privates Yates 2 & Nuttall J.T. of 177 Coy. These were the only casualties incurred by the company.	405 cm
	20/3/17		Fine weather continues.	
			177 Company relieved by 175th Coy between 10 am & 1 pm, the relief was carried out without a stream over.	

WAR DIARY / INTELLIGENCE SUMMARY

Army Form C. 2118.

Place	Date	Hour	Summary of Events and Information	Remarks and references to Appendices

Lindi	20/3/17		Contd.
			16 Boer 2 am (rear attack)
			18 Deter 5 am (front attack)
			4 very severely & shot both captain.
			4 Lewis gun.
			An exchange of filled belts there was effected.
			177 Company packed Red Camp at Faechemual at 4 am. There existed 2 kits.
			The total rounds of ammunition fired by 177 Coy during their period in the line was:—
			    No. 1 Section 4 guns 8435 Rds
			         2 4750
			         3 3500
			         4 9450
			                   Total 26,135 Rds
			The troops were either S.O.S. on the Company sector, the Company was actually in the trenches 14 days.
				original

Lovemound	21/3/17		Fadden hut fires, road drying. Company spent the day in cleaning up, bring clothing, guns to each section. 3 very pain Lewis in new palm boots were issued to the following orders were received by the O/C 177 M/G Coy:—	Wilson

Army Form C. 2118.

WAR DIARY
or
INTELLIGENCE SUMMARY
(Erase heading not required.)

Original

Instructions regarding War Diaries and Intelligence Summaries are contained in F.S. Regs., Part II. and the Staff Manual respectively. Title Pages will be prepared in manuscript.

Place	Date	Hour	Summary of Events and Information	Remarks and references to Appendices
Toucancourt	21/3/17		"The Company is to be congratulated on having no cases of trench feet" the O/C wishes to recognise the good behaviour & cheerful spirit of the men of the Company, the majority of whom were under fire for the first time during this tour, the trenches were in a bad state (chest deep in mud), in that respect. He OC hopes this spirit will remain the abovequoted paragraph was abstracted from 177 Inf.Coy. will continue unimpaired conditions.	W3 cm
Toucancourt	22/3/17		Snow on the early morning Operation Parade 9.30 — new tunic officer Day — 11.30 Luncheon — 12.30 pm Berthing — 2.30 (shot hotels) The men were issued with new shirt, pants, socks, vest found in apology for old. A bundle of pay held at Toucancourt found that the excited rehashed under date 19 were accidental no blame attaching to any individual.	
Toucancourt	23/3/17		A fine day following a frosty night. After the 9.30 on parade the employer worked repeated Limbers under leisten officer's supervision. 191 Y. employing the service of no one applies to a QM stores	67 cm

2449 Wt. W14957/M90 750,000 1/16 J.B.C. & A. Forms/C.2118/12.

WAR DIARY or INTELLIGENCE SUMMARY

Army Form C. 2118.

Place	Date	Hour	Summary of Events and Information	Remarks and references to Appendices
Forceville	23/3/17		Contd. that is a company in the parade ground, afterwards everything to blow in absolute[ly] pre-war style. As quickly as the supplies received if it means all to wear of this material amounted to £30 directly, other than for the material amounted to £30 directly, might be better employed. Capt Sharp is in charge by Corp. N.S.P. Cold N.E. wind.	5.30 a.m.
	24/3/17	10 a.m.	Co inspected the company regards cleanness of clothing, accoutrements, equipment &c. Still N.E. wind, in full marching order. Afternoon Section Officers inspected rifles, revolvers, haversacks. Men fell in for a short route march. In the afternoon the company were drilled in the use of gas respirators under lecture by Section Officers. Capt Gaffney went to Brigade at 10-0 a.m. He received orders for inspection tomorrow. Subject to the following we have to report to 2nd Army. Weather fine — NE wind.	W/S Capt
	25/3/17		Brigadier inspected annually. Inspection by Section officer. No 3 Section packed limbers at 9.30 a.m. + moved off at 10 a.m. to LE MESNIL via Bertrancourt, Louvencourt, Acheux, Candas, Beauval, Gezaincourt. Arrived 3.30 p.m. + immediately took over billets from 143 Lys Coy.	W/S Capt

Army Form C. 2118.

WAR DIARY
INTELLIGENCE SUMMARY
(Erase heading not required.)

Army Form C. 2118.

Original

Place	Date	Hour	Summary of Events and Information	Remarks and references to Appendices
Touncourt	26/3/17		Operations received N.E. wind rained at intervals during the day. Received orders to stand by for immediate move at 10:30 a.m. At noon received orders to move to Etarpigny at once. Report to Brigade. Company headed moved off at 1:30 p.m. to Etarpigny via Eben, Agencidin, Boulant. Arrived Etarpigny at 4:45 p.m. parked limbers & picketed mules. Men were billeted in the village.	
Etarpigny	27/3/17		Early morning fine wind cold N.E. wind. Later in the day rain. Received Brigade orders at 12:45 a.m. to stand by to move at short notice to be kind of Batarguy. Received orders to move at 10:30 a.m. to 4 hrivid. Company moved off immediately. Arrived at 4. Received 12 noon. 4 Regt then with operation orders received at 3 pm No. 14 & 15 from moved off at 4:45 p.m. to report to 5th Lincoln. Met Lincolns respectively to take up outpost line. Weather fine – at 6 rained. Later in the day showing to little rain.	4/5 aup
Lebonois	28/3/17		Brigade orders received 12:30 a.m. Orders to move to Hargocourt	Nr2 Cm

WAR DIARY
INTELLIGENCE SUMMARY

Army Form C. 2118.

(Erase heading not required.)

(13) Instructions regarding War Diaries and Intelligence Summaries are contained in F.S. Regs., Part II. and the Staff Manual respectively. Title Pages will be prepared in manuscript.

Onnyround

Place	Date	Hour	Summary of Events and Information	Remarks and references to Appendices
Le Mesnil	28/3/17		No 3 Lewis gun withdrawn from Le Mesnil. Company less No 3 Section marched off at 11.0 a.m. to Hancourt via Estrées leaving rearguard 12.30 p.m. Field company formed advanced guard. Prepared to hold ability for the night No 2 & 3 Section packed & in billets with light fighting load stood by to move at a moments notice.	W5 Coy
Hancourt	29/3/17		Weather cloudy showery occasional intervals of sunshine. Company arrived with rations 12.30 pm. Rations taken to Do. Instructions at NESBECOURT FARM & ROISEL. Left guns in the ROISEL defences fixed at small parties of Germans in the direction of NESBECOURT abeveatin was suffered Retaliation with h.g. fire followed with a few minutes but shots went high. Two additional guns to repair Brigade order received 19 pm. additional guns to OC 5th Lincolns on 30th to OC 1st Lincolns.	W6 Coy
Hancourt	30/3/17		S.W. wind showery all day with intervals of sunshine. Capt. Shepherd rode the Brigade HQ Godegnies for No 2 Section. Section reported to OC 5th Lincolns at 9.30 am. at 10 am	

2449 Wt. W14957/M90 750,000 1/16 J.B.C. & A. Forms/C.2118/12.

WAR DIARY

INTELLIGENCE SUMMARY

Army Form C. 2118.

Original

Place	Date	Hour	Summary of Events and Information	Remarks and references to Appendices
Manancourt	30/3/17		Cont. No. 3 Section officer reported to O.C. & Lincolns received orders not to bring his guns into position according to Brigade orders until level movement of No.3 section cancelled until further orders at 10 a.m. Capt. Sheffield arrived back from Brigade conference at 11 am with information re attack on Hermilly, Haubécourt, Hill 140 on the 31st inst. No machine guns section to at 2 pm Co. 5 Lincoln, Capt. Sheffield & 2Lt. Heronicles out to reconnoitre ground for attack. No. 3 Section moved off at 8 pm for Russel	
Manancourt	31/3/17		Weather changeable - dry wind - showery with frequent intervals of bright sunshine. Orders received 10.30 am from Brigade through Capt. Sheffield to make barrage fire during artillery bombardment preceding attack on Hermilly & Heudicourt. No. 3 Section accompanied attacking force.	

WAR DIARY

INTELLIGENCE SUMMARY

Army Form C. 2118.

Place	Date	Hour	Summary of Events and Information	Remarks and references to Appendices
Havrincourt	31/8/17	6 a.m.	No. 1 Section had 1 gun gave covering fire to attacking troops from position near Road. No. 1 Section gave barrage & gave covering fire from high ground S.W. of Hermies. No. 2 Section were held in reserve at Havrincourt. Operations were completely successful. We suffered no casualties during the attack.	W.M. w/p

[signatures]

M.F. Ruffhead Capt
Adj. 177 Coy R.E.

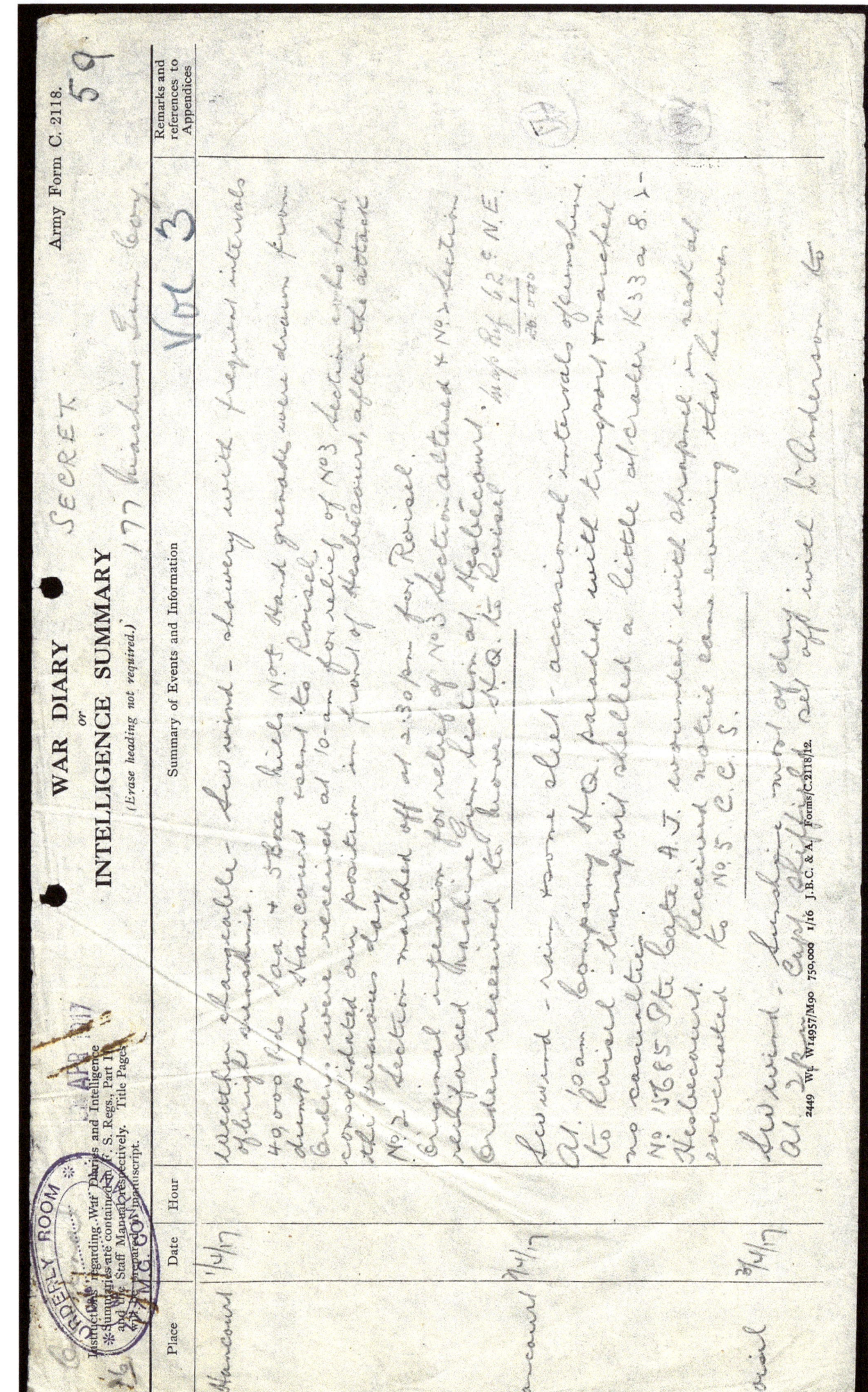

WAR DIARY or INTELLIGENCE SUMMARY

Army Form C. 2118.

177 Machine Gun Coy

Vol 3

Place	Date	Hour	Summary of Events and Information	Remarks and references to Appendices
Harcourt	1/4/17		Weather changeable - low wind - showery with frequent intervals of bright sunshine. 40,000 S.A.A. + 3 Boxes Mills Nº 5 Hand grenades were drawn from dump in Harcourt sent to Roisel. Orders were received at 10 a.m. for relief of Nº 3 Section. Nº 2 Section consolidated our position in front of Heubecourt, after the attack the previous day. Nº 2 Section marched off at 2.30 p.m. for Roisel. Original intention for relief of Nº 3 Section altered & Nº 2 Section retired towards S.W. section of Heubecourt. Orders received to move S.H.Q. to Roisel. Map Ref 62ᶜ N.E. 1/20000	
Harcourt	2/4/17		Low wind - rainy morning clear - occasional intervals of sunshine. At 10 a.m. Company H.Q. paraded with transport marched to Roisel. Transport shelled a little at crater K33a 8.1 - No casualties. Nº 13665 Pte Capt. A.J. examined with shrapnel in neck at Heubecourt. Received notice same evening that he was evacuated to Nº 5. C.C.S.	
Roisel	3/4/17		Low wind - sunshine most of day. At 2 p.m. Capt. Killick [?] set off with 1st Anderson to	

WAR DIARY or **INTELLIGENCE SUMMARY**   Army Form C. 2118.

(17) Machine Gun Coy

Place	Date	Hour	Summary of Events and Information	Remarks and references to Appendices
Raial	3/4/17	cont'd	reconnoitre ground for attack & start for 9.30pm. Visited Col. Johnson at 4pm who desired to keep M.G. Section in reserve until objective had been gained. Capt. Sheffield returned 8.30pm. As the infantry failed to take their objective the M.G.s did not advance.	Rain
Raial	4/4/17		Fresh wind - snowed all day. At 9.30am a H.E. shell bursting outside a shelter in Headquarters occupied by No 2 Section wounded & or killed 1108 gunners. The following is a list of casualties:— 53339 Hope Smelly. D n 59376 Ota Pitcalvin 59376 Dawber E 1347 Dunsley W. (attacker) One of the casualties went to a dressing station. One team & gun of No. 4 Section went to replace gun + casualties in No. 1 Section. Arrived at Raial from Hebecourt farm at 3.30pm.	

Army Form C. 2118.

WAR DIARY
or
INTELLIGENCE SUMMARY

Secret.

(Erase heading not required.) 177 Machine Gun Company

Original

Instructions regarding War Diaries and Intelligence Summaries are contained in F.S. Regs., Part II. and the Staff Manual respectively. Title Pages will be prepared in manuscript.

Place	Date	Hour	Summary of Events and Information	Remarks and references to Appendices
Ervillers	4/4/17		Both Reliefs up with return limbers by relieving No 3 section. Relief completed at 9.15 pm. No 3 section returned to Rocquigny. No 2 section took up a defensive line in rear of Lempire.	ApplX
Ervillers	5/4/17		Low wind - sunshine all day. Transport moved from previous line on account of shell fire. No 2 section took up a defensive line in front of Lempire. Two guns of No 1 section helped to consolidate a front of Lempire.	
Ervillers	6/4/17		Fine weather - sunshine all day. At 2.30pm 5740 Pte Zorba W. was wounded at the neck by H.E. fragment. Reported at Company H.Q. later to 178th Field Ambulance. In the evening Capt. Allfrey went to Lempire on reconnaissance. At 6.30 pm whilst watching the guns, H.E. shell wounded	

2449 Wt. W14957/M90 750,000 1/16 J.B.C. & A. Forms/C.2118/12.

WAR DIARY or INTELLIGENCE SUMMARY

Army Form C. 2118.

APR 1917

177 Machine Gun Coy

Place	Date	Hour	Summary of Events and Information	Remarks and references to Appendices
Roisel	6/4/17		Gentil 2/Lt Calvert. E. Killed. 46178 Sgt. Thorpe C.E. and 58518 Pte Jennings E5. No 3 section guns were taken over by 2/Lt Stemmons and 2/Lt Calvert's body was taken to field dressing station.	M.M.M
Roisel	7/4/17		Fine weather - smoke all day. No 3 section pushed limbers in readiness to move to Templeux for attack on Berracque Farm. Operation orders postponed 24 hours by telephone message from Brigade. 7.0 pm O.C. No 3 section with officers of 375 Divn reconnoitred ground for attack. Operation orders above mentioned received further notice.	M.M.M
Roisel	8/4/17		Fine weather. 2 M stores moved to Roisel 2.30 No 3 section paraded marched off to Templeux to relieve No 2 section No 2 section were relieved by gun teams, the relief being completed at 10 pm.	M.M.M

Army Form C. 2118.

WAR DIARY
or
INTELLIGENCE SUMMARY
(Erase heading not required.)

Original   Secret

20   177 Machine Gun Coy

APR 1917

Instructions regarding War Diaries and Intelligence Summaries are contained in F. S. Regs., Part II. and the Staff Manual respectively. Title Pages will be prepared in manuscript.

Place	Date	Hour	Summary of Events and Information	Remarks and references to Appendices
Roeux	9/4/17		Cold wind – a little snow. Capt. Sheffield visited Brigade for information re coming attack on Serapus Farm German trench. Lecture fired by O.O. during the day re disposition of machine gun. During the day Germans evacuated our objectives expecting our advance to occupy same. Machine guns were pushed forward to consolidate the gains.	
Roeux	10/4/17		Cold wind – a little snow. Capt. Sheffield went up the line & reinforced the new defense line with more M.G's.	
Roeux	11/4/17		Cold wind – snow. Capt. Sheffield went up to line with a view to reorganize M.G. defense – returned 2.30 p.m. At 4 p.m. Board of Inquiry was held re the loss of a mule from the kraal on April 1st. Finding – not due to neglect. Brigade order re two M.G.'s in Brigade to be fitted for Aeroplane firing complete except one gun from No.1 Division & gun from No.1 Section details for this purpose. At 3.35 p.m. hostile aeroplane above emplacements for	

WAR DIARY
INTELLIGENCE SUMMARY

Army Form C. 2118.

Place	Date	Hour	Summary of Events and Information	Remarks and references to Appendices
Roisel	11/4/17		Both Aeroplanes bringing map were wounded by shrapnel:- 59.50 O.Pts Lieut N & 57391 - Wallis J.	NWS
Roisel	12/4/17		Lieut Hillcot reported at Company HQ from Etaples. Weather mycold, wind strong NW, showery. From 5 to 7pm heavy fall of snow. Capt Sheffield & Lt Hillcot visited gun position to left of Zenaghi Farm where new position behind enemy river L16 a.50.40 & L10 b.72 L10 c.8.2. Capt Sheffield returned to Brigade HQ. all the HQ implacements were visited. Enemy were seen moving in trenches at F29 & F29 c.10.50. Two guns tried up new position LL2 c.30.90 & L16 c.40.10. No 2 Sections guns in charge of Jn Carlisle. Between 10 & 1am one of our Aeroplanes was forced to land at L20.c. It was attacked by two enemy aircraft, one of our airmen being wounded. Our machine was shelled by enemy artillery & badly damaged. No 4 Section came out for heat being relieved by No 2 Section.	NWS
Roisel	13/4/17		Weather very fine. Capt Sheffield & Lt Hillcot went ruinnies Nw to by Ries Hoilget Observation positions the edge of ridge. position located Several - Dugouts for night firing. no for rain	

WAR DIARY or INTELLIGENCE SUMMARY

Army Form C. 2118

Original 177 Machine Gun Coy

Place	Date	Hour	Summary of Events and Information	Remarks and references to Appendices
Ruitz	13/4/17		The gun position to the left of Fevague Farm were changed, one gun being placed at L.23.d.30.30 & one at L.16.c.40.10. Heywood went over No. 2 Section's guns & Turbaluch returned to his own section. Large amount of smoke was seen behind enemy lines slightly S.E. of Bois Wood & two heavy explosions. Limit column of black smoke. Four enemy aircraft came over between 6 & 7 p.m. Enemy shelled Fevague Farm & little Pl L.4.a.90.50, very little shelling by enemy artillery. No guns anti-aircraft fired on enemy planes.	
Ruitz	14/4/17		Weather fine & very sunshine. Capt. Oldfield & [?] billet visited Ban Riel & obtained L.23.a 40.30 to give M.G. fire support to [?] of M Section attacking cottage at L.23.d. 70.80. M Section visited all gun positions to left of Fevague Farm also M.G. emplacements prepared for night of 15 inst.	
Ruitz	15/4/17		Weather cloudy with occasional showers towards evening, very windy & unsettling strong N.W. breeze in evening. Capt. Oldfield visited to guns & rear at 9.30 a.m. Ban Biel gun No 1. M billet over to H.G. to left of Fevague Farm also visited O.C. & S Section at Neuville replenished L.G.	

2449 Wt. W14957/Mgo 750,000 1/16 J.B.C. & A. Forms/C.2118/12.

War Diary / Intelligence Summary

Army Form C. 2118

Original — 17 Machine Gun Coy

23

Place	Date	Hour	Summary of Events and Information	Remarks and references to Appendices
Roeux	19/4/17	Both	Position to support 9th Lancers attack on Millerit. 8 M Guns were placed in position to create barrage fire between the tall railway sign QUARRY & MILLERT. Range from 1000 to 1700 yards. 9th Lancers attacked at 9.30 pm. Mr. Guns opened fire at 11.45 pm to 12.45 am. One casualty (Pte Lauren) about 1 am. 6,050 rounds. Sandbagging from HQ. Front line hit with H.E. but were apparently unharmed and to 5 guns shrapnel was used at 3.30 am many of 16th & 9th. Lancers reported for duty from HQ base.	NWW
Roeux	16/4/17		Weather cold. Heavy showers wind strong. N.W. & W. No 4 section relieved. No 1 section of 9 Bn. Lt. Yout went on duty with N.4. section. Capt. Duffield went to Brigade Orders for conference. Several general mortars were transported down.	NWW
Roeux	17/4/17		Gospels westerly wind. Millerit Farm fell. Heavy enemy occupied. CRE made a tour of Roeux & the country to Windmill with view of using NEWS & OC Newts. Frontline trench every part for Mr Gs to support	

2449 Wt. W14957/M90 750,000 1/16 J.B.C. & A. Forms/C.2118/12.

WAR DIARY or INTELLIGENCE SUMMARY

Army Form C. 2118.

APR 1917

Place: Roiral / Riviere / 17 Machine Gun Coy

Place	Date	Hour	Summary of Events and Information	Remarks and references to Appendices
Roiral	17/4/17		Contd. attack on Enemy. 8 Guns to creep barrage to left of QUARRY & 4 guns fire in relieve to move forward if required to support the after consolidating.	
Roiral	18/4/17		Weather cloudy & considerable amount of rainfall. OC & Major Liddle 175 Coy visited the M.G positions to relief on the 20 inst. Two section officers of 175 Coy also visited M.G positions	
Roiral	19/4/17		Weather rained & very windy since N.W & N.winds. preventing observation. OC went to Bde HQrs Rivol No.1 melee S.W. Lincoln to arrange for M.G. support in the attack on the QUARRY. Town HP of No.4 section were moved forward to the finale alongs the M.G. were not to await orders & as I was sgnoled the HP had been taken up by the enemy to support the posts that had been taken up by the attacking infantry. The HP retired to their former defence line position. The other HP were held in readiness to make a barrage fire on the left of QUARRY & own other HP to barrage the west to the right of QUARRY & under of the barrage fires were required	

WAR DIARY
or
INTELLIGENCE SUMMARY.
(Erase heading not required.)

Army Form C. 2118.

Original   177 Machine Gun Coy

APR 1917

Place	Date	Hour	Summary of Events and Information	Remarks and references to Appendices
Enurel	25/4/17		Weather cloudy, wind warm. Strong wind NW & N but the company showed by 175 MGC relief carried out in good order, all action relieved by 4 pm. The Company moved to Bruay to Brigade Rest. The Company moved to Bruires out timber transport open. COMS company cars.	LWW
Bruires	26/4/17		Weather cloudy but dry, wind fresh W to NW, company in rest. Two AA aircraft guns were mounted, old cart wheels being used for the purpose, which prove very satisfactory for this purpose. Company paraded at 9am under section officers were inspected & cleaning guns annexes to. Lectures made to drivers & incited, all ranks inspire be hold out with from section officers worker by officers. One replacement conducted as a defence lie to, balm - stretcher maneuver.	LWW
Bruires	27/4/17		Weather fine with great NW wind. The company supplied 5omm + 5NCOs for fatigue overhead transport Major GE. Major Grant under order Lieut B E ~ were mounted for anti aircraft work.	

(A7091). Wt. W12830/M1203 75,000. 1/17. D. D. & L., Ltd. Forms/C.2118/14.

WAR DIARY
or
INTELLIGENCE SUMMARY.

Army Form C. 2118.

Place	Date	Hour	Summary of Events and Information	Remarks and references to Appendices
Berne	27/4/17		Observation balloon was destroyed by enemy aeroplane between 9.30 & 10 am. H.Q. opened fire & enemy aeroplane was in very close proximity to balloon before fire had to be stopped. The remainder of the company paraded at 6 am & was employed cleaning guns & equipment. From 9 to 10 am enemy shell fell in Berne	
Berne	23/4/17		Weather very fine with fresh N.W. wind. The company was paraded at 9 am under the O.C. Clothing & equipment, Box respirators, P.H. helmets & sim (?) latrines were carefully inspected. Remainder of day was spent in cleaning ammn, belts, spare parts, packing limbers. Five enemy aircraft were seen S.E. of Berne, they were engaged by our A.A. aircraft between 7.30 & 8.30. Between 7.30 pm there was a scrap between an aircraft close of the ext(?) of this aircraft came down to investigate, apparently in a collision both pilots killed. The third biplane came down on fire & crashed on plowed land at east of LE' VERGUIER, pilot & observer escaped.	
Berne	28/4/17		Weather fine with wind N to SW wind. The company took a 3 in't NCO to report upon Turnfler(?) between (?) the afternoon of the company employed in defence of approach of the company. 6.30 – 7.30 pm C.P.T. 1st. 9/10 GJ under Lieut. Officer, the new crew colored(?) mechanism, gunoil & I.A. from 2 – 4 am drill exchg, cleaning gun & spare parts.	

WAR DIARY

Army Form C. 2118.

Kent

17 Machine Gun Coy

(1) Bapaume

Place	Date	Hour	Summary of Events and Information	Remarks and references to Appendices
Bapaume	14/4/17		All ranks collected property treated morning heat & went — weather fine & bright. Company paraded at 9.0am under O.C. & marched to parade ground 1 mile west of Bapaume & being hot the men stamped & were thrown up for inspection by the Brigadier. At 10am Brigadier Major arrived & inspected the company, all rifle & revolver equipment, ammunition, etc. Section was served in good full range gun fire was tested. The company marched past the Brigadier who complimented the O.C. officers & the men very heartily upon their smart soldierly appearance, also on the good manner the bulk of the equipment & the transport were complimented on the mules, horses.	
Bapaume	15/4/17		Weather fine, fresh breeze from N.W. Officer i/c No 4 Section with 12 men conducted two h.c. emplacements at posts 15 & 17 in Beaume-Hamicourt. Raised defence scheme. Remainder of Company resting. O.C. visited H.Q. of 17th h.s. Coy to arrange relief & make a long tour of all the machine gun positions & posts in front — reverse. Enemy artillery very active during the night.	

(A7092). Wt. W12839/M1293. 75,000. 1/17. D. D. & L., Ltd. Forms/C.2118-14.

WAR DIARY
INTELLIGENCE SUMMARY

Army Form C. 2118.

APR 1917

Original — 177 Machine Gun Coy

Place	Date	Hour	Summary of Events and Information	Remarks and references to Appendices
Bruce	27/4/17		Weather cloudy cold, fresh wind N to NW. 12 TM under Lt. Barkly did some work on H.Q. position in the Station Ravine, started final defence scheme. 2 in command attached as gunnery officer to the village of Bruce, was relieved from 9 to 10.30 by order. 5. Still direct falling quite near H.Q. any killed. Relief of H.Q. C.174 postponed for 24 hours.	
Bruce	28/4/17		Weather cloudy in morning sun broke out at 9.30 am, wind breeze from N to NE. Company paraded at H.Q. 9.30 am. Lieutenant also O.C. Inspection of arms & ammunition, morning 10 to 1.15 spent on arms & ammunition. 1 A + gun drill. 2 Co H.Q. parties labour. 2 in command toured area of 174 H.Q.Coy. Final arrangements for relief of 174 H.Q.Coy.	
Bruce	29/4/17		No 3 Section paraded N.E. and marched, gun recovery Tara to move to Villers-en-Cauchies will 174 H.Q. H.Q.T. JEANCOURT.	

Original
Secret

WAR DIARY
or
INTELLIGENCE SUMMARY
(Erase heading not required.)

177 M.G. Coy

April / 1917

Army Form C. 2118.

Place	Date	Hour	Summary of Events and Information	Remarks and references to Appendices

Berles	29/4/17		Cont¹
			Military N°4 Section at 11 am on reserve.
			N°1 Section 177 Coy relieved N°2 Section 174 Coy 1:45 p/m
			  2 " 177 " " " " 174 " 3:30
			  4 " 177 " " " " 174 " 5:30
			
			At present there are 8 M.G. in support of the Brigade Infantry posts from where M.G. positions are being constructed. 12 M.G. will be in support of the infantry during the day. There are four M.G.s on anti-aircraft defence. Two guns N°2 Section at GRAN RIEL WOODS engaged enemy rifle pits at L.24.a.6.8. where movement of enemy was observed.	

Ervrenet	30/4/17		Weather fine during N.E. hazy evening. O.C. visited the whole of M.G. on Brigade frontage. Reconnoitred new positions which are now under construction. Two of our guns were moved to the left i.e. one at L.23.c.1.7. Two at L.23 a.8. & 4. 200 M.G. Coy. Two guns relieved those of the 20th MG. Coy. The enemy were quiet along the Brigade front, occasional shelling	16 2nd Middlesex Cph Lt 177 M.G.C.

CR/6/14/4
Army Form C. 2118.

177th MACHINE GUN COY
WAR DIARY
INTELLIGENCE SUMMARY.

(Erase heading not required.)

MAY 1917

Instructions regarding War Diaries and Intelligence Summaries are contained in F. S. Regs., Part II. and the Staff Manual respectively. Title pages will be prepared in manuscript.

Place	Date	Summary of Events and Information	Remarks and references to Appendices
Jeancourt	15/5/17	Weather fine bright sun, wind N.E. fresh breeze. Aeroplanes at 10 a.m. enemy were seen engaged in band control east of JEANCOURT they were two of ours. OC visited M.G. at front line defences at 10.5. at 9 h.up 21.6.5.S.E. a concealed gun pit patrol & position reconnoitred & a long hill running to center to M.G. position (mounting a gun 15 th they were being from during afternoon. M.G. fired on small group at Q.19.b.6.7 also on enemy were seen working enemy were also seen at Q.14.b.6.3 were fired on by M.G.S. Ammunition expended 1500 rounds. Two enemy M.G.s were mounted on cart wheels at Coy JHQ JEANCOURT L.26.a.8.6	J.O.L.t
Jeancourt	16/5/17	Weather bright sun, fresh breeze N.E. dangerous. OC visited M.G. position. stationary attacks & M.G. position. Wald done. Reconnoitred made at the following points (Chapnet 62.SE) R.15.d.9.8, L.34.b.2.4. M.G. positions were examined and every effort being made by sentries by the enemy was made by every thing behind ridges G.14.6.a. at 10.15 & 11.30 p.m. Train going East behind ridges G.14.6.a. reporting & the enemy reinforcements by railway were noticed.	

Ground of fortress range dep 4/5
M.G.S. { G.18 c.2.5 — 1,500
       { G.13 b.5.4 — 2,500
       { G.14 c.6.5 — 500
       { G.14 c.7. — 500
AIRCRAFT — 200

Coro R2. a. and Co No 2 sec.

Appt. W1. w12830/M492 700000/1/17. D. D. & L., Ltd. Forms/C21871a.

WAR DIARY
or
INTELLIGENCE SUMMARY.

(Erase heading not required.)

Army Form C. 2118.

Place	Date	Summary of Events and Information	Remarks and references to Appendices
Lincourt	3/5/17	Bright bush. wind W to N.w. changing afternoon to N.W.E. O.C. + 2 i/c formed raised M.G's front line trenches. M.G. position at L.35.a.2.4 + L.35.a.13.0 (Map Ref 62dSE) front position with field of fire to right. 2nd A covered emplacement was made at L.22.c.9.5. with 8mm aperture line. Other M.G. position improved + covered from aerial observation. Firing Dogs. M.G's Target Range Lead Sup Remarks 2 { G.32.6.6.4 } 1,800 500 } Guns were used by enemy. { G.32.6.5.8 } } 2 to 4 am 4 { G.14.c.8.0 } 2,200 } Covered to { G.7.d.9.0 } 2,500 } 6,500 } attack of } Colegne Farm + Khidloff 2 { G.14.c.6.3 } 2,000 } Farm { G.14.c. Lecoul } 2,000 } 4,000 1 Aircraft 500	MM
Lincourt	4/5/17	Bright sunshine with mild breeze W to N.W. O.C. visited M.G's front line defences + at 9.30 p.m. was with officer i/c No 2 detach with a reconnaissance party of t.2.4.6 to locate forward M.G positions to fire on BLISSON FARM G.14.6. Used direct sighting today / M.G emplacements made south end of	

Army Form C. 2118.

WAR DIARY
or
INTELLIGENCE SUMMARY.

(Erase heading not required.)

Place	Date	Summary of Events and Information	Remarks and references to Appendices
Jeancourt	4/5/17	GRAND PRIEL WOODS + 30 others commenced at L.34.6.7.6. L.35.a.3.0 L.35.a.3.0 & L.35.a.3.0 (both L.6.e.S.E). Firing front. MGs — Target — Range — Rds. app. 4 AIRCRAFT 400 1 CUCKOO 2,500 500 About 5 stops out of our observation balloons were brought down during day. Them all friendly by enemy aircraft.	MM
Jeancourt	5/5/17	Bright weather, very hot during the day. Wind N. to S.W. fresh breeze. The enemy attacked our outposts at G.32 Central own S.O.S. was used. The M.G.s opened fire on them S.O.S. line at 10.45 p.m. Jam used 8,000 rds. Firing. MGs — Target — Range — Rds. 2 GRIDER 2,500 750 2 AIRCRAFT 200	
Jeancourt	6/5/17	Bright sun very hot went first to bge. N.E. O.C. trials M.G. positions ed'd Brigade Major. Ward done. M.G. covered experiments were improved gun splinter proof cover made.	MM

WAR DIARY
or
INTELLIGENCE SUMMARY

Army Form C. 2118.

(33)

Place	Date	Hour	Summary of Events and Information	Remarks and references to Appendices
Jeancourt	6/5/17		Gen¹ Firing Target Range Ammo Exp 2 C14c8> 2000 750 2 Aircraft — 300 Officer ch'g No. 4 Section of MGs with Reps 10th Company on our right tricked their HQ position so as pre-arranged got to work arranged the guns of 177th & 10th MG Coy should the no. 4 placed so as to find up the two units. the dispositions of guns are good.	✓
Jeancourt	7/5/17		Bright sun, wind dangerous N to NE. Wind dg¹⁰ No 3 Section officers at 8.0 am made a reconnaissance of ground at L.18 Central with object of locating MG position. Farm occupied by enemy at C14 C.B>. MG position were sighted that afternoon a working party proceeded to the position located, deepened old occupied trenches prepared open MG position. Firing 3 M Gs over to Vequies & Jeancourt Aircraft 10.000 sn	✓
Jeancourt	8/5/17		Rain during the morn⁹, cloudy wind fresh W. to N.W. F.G.C.M. at Jeancourt Pct Willett member of the court	

Army Form C. 2118.

WAR DIARY
INTELLIGENCE SUMMARY.
(Erase heading not required.)

Place	Date	Summary of Events and Information	Remarks and references to Appendices
Fampoux	8/5/17	Quiet. Pte Hixon a/95 Leicester Regt (T.F.) attacked 177460 was brought up to trial. Major Sheffield &. Bolland, Lieut Helpen, witnesses. 2/Lt. Heymann Prosecutor. Work done :— H.Q. splinter proof implement made at L22.c.9.5 (new 6.2°N.E.) covered up. S.ft. long made to this position from the trench. M.G. Position at L23.a.18 made splinter proof, stood drained. Enemy artillery quiet.	nil
Fampoux	9/5/17	Weather cloudy & showers. Wind N. to N.E. O.C. visited all M.G. positions in Front line defences. Work done :— H.Q. position commenced at L34.a central in Brown line after scheme. M.G. position L28 about completed. 15 braces S.A.A. sent to ration HQ at L22.d.28 & taken to Section HQ at R9.a.57. Firing done:— M.G. Target Range San Kennels L35.c.63 Brown mds. Brown & Postcard 2 C33 a 39 3400 1500 Points used by enemy at night.	nil

Army Form C. 2118.

WAR DIARY
or
INTELLIGENCE SUMMARY.
(Erase heading not required.)

Place	Date	Summary of Events and Information	Remarks and references to Appendices
Jeancourt	19/5/17	Fine weather, bright sun, wind N.W to N.W. Work done — H.G. position at L23.C.15.85 has been completed. Trench splinter proof concealed. Firing done — Nil. 6 Boxes S.A.A sent to No 1 Section	
Jeancourt	11/5/17	Bright sun, wind fresh to N.E to N.E. OC visited Brown defence line. Located 6 M.G. & alternative positions. These positions were commenced & necessary material collected for construction. Firing done — M. Gs Target San Remark L35.F.6.3) G33.a.3.9 1500 x Bursts used by enemy at night 2 Aircraft 800 Flying over Jeancourt Enemy H.G. fired at our trenches L23.a.5.5. OC 177 & OC 14 squadron M.M.G cavalry made a tour of H.G. positions	
Jeancourt	17/5/17	Weather - bright sun. OC visited Brown H.G. positions. Work done — The H.G. positions located at Le Reguirer & Peumel Wood were carried on at night	Cont.

WAR DIARY
or
INTELLIGENCE SUMMARY
(Erase heading not required)

Army Form C. 2118.

Place	Date	Summary of Events and Information	Remarks and references to Appendices
Fencourt	1/5/17	Boches firing done target Lea. 2 MG's aircraft 500. At 3 pm several explosions were heard near the vicinity of Potzroux, at 12 midnight fires were observed upon town. Patrol felt M G was brought down by enemy As a gun.	
Fencourt	2/5/17	Weather bright, enemy normal. N E G E heavy shown from 8.15 4 pm. Gun changes to W + N by Line Officer. He NCO's from the 14th 15CE harried M G Coveney tradition used at M G Garrison persons to what length at the 17 coy MG dug outs. Were done. The new M G position under construction were preserved.	
Fencourt	3/5/17	Fine bright day, GC rode a talk of MC persons in company of 13 the Kursulhy M. D. Guo C.O. loosding, Lieu M G experienced complexity in the Browns debours bin, there were several explosions showed in the enemy lines, apparently destroying dugouts. Lieu Milbut attached as a number of NC o M held at JEONCOURT at 2 pm	

Army Form C. 2118.

WAR DIARY
or
INTELLIGENCE SUMMARY.
(Erase heading not required.)

Instructions regarding War Diaries and Intelligence Summaries are contained in F.S. Regs., Part II. and the Staff Manual respectively. Title pages will be prepared in manuscript.

37

Place	Date	Summary of Events and Information	Remarks and references to Appendices
Fencourt	15/5/17	Fresh wind NE to E. The Company was relieved by 13th & 14th Cavalry M.G. Squadrons. No 2 Section — No 3 — 2 guns No 1 Section } relieved by 13th Sqdn en on 3.30, 4.30 & 5 p.m. No 4 Section 2 guns No 1 Section } relieved by 1st Sqdn on at 12.30/1 am morning of 16 inst. The Company were billeted at VRAIGNES occupying Billets Nos 50 & 52.	XVII
Vraignes	16/5/17	Heavy rain during the day. Day programme of work:- Cleaning billets & general went pretty lavish cleaning guns & gun parts.	XVIII
Vraignes	17/5/17	Weather cloudy & damp Day programme of work. 9 — 12 Cleaning billets, erection of ablution stand, incinerators & latrines. 2 — 4 Cleaning equipment, clothing etc. The transport were removed from HANCOURT & Vraignes stabled in other No 44.	XVIII
Vraignes	18/5/17	Bugle am Company programme of work 9 – 12 Cleaning guns & cleaning equipment	

Army Form C. 2118.

WAR DIARY
or
INTELLIGENCE SUMMARY.
(Erase heading not required.)

38

Instructions regarding War Diaries and Intelligence
Summaries are contained in F. S. Regs., Part II.
and the Staff Manual respectively. Title pages
will be prepared in manuscript.

Place	Date	Summary of Events and Information	Remarks and references to Appendices
Troupes	18/5/17	Parts 2-3p. Lecture drill price arms 3- '' - Lecture - Discipline	
Troupes	19/5/17	Brigham reg. td. Coy Parade at 6-30 to 7-30 am. P.T. 9 - 12.30 17/9 Bn Redoin drill 2 - 4pm Cooling Lecture	
Troupes	20/5/17	Bright any cloudy in afternoon, slight thunder storm to N.E. Brigade Church Parade at P. 15 a. at 10 am. 177 bn Football Team played 175 coy at Bruan. 175 coy won 2-1. tie. 14 bugles were isolated suffering from a small rash that had been found inside the jacket. It appears this is a case from an offence N.Y.D	
Troupes	21/5/17	Weather cloudy, heavy rain during the day. Programme of work. 6.30 - 7.30 am P.T. 9 - 12.30 2 - 4pm Bren drill, musketry in attack, washing timber, timber carrying.	

WAR DIARY
or
INTELLIGENCE SUMMARY.
(Erase heading not required.)

Army Form C. 2118.

Original diary

Instructions regarding War Diaries and Intelligence Summaries are contained in F.S. Regs., Part II. and the Staff Manual respectively. Title pages will be prepared in manuscript.

Place	Date	Hour	Summary of Events and Information	Remarks and references to Appendices
Khargpur	21/5/17		Bright sun. Programme of work:- 6.30 – 7.30 am P.T. under section officers. 9.30 – 12.30 I.A. Gun + Infantry Drill. 2 – 4 pm Sports + P.T.	Initials
Khargpur	23/5/17		Considerable rain fell during the day. Programme of work:- 6.30 to 7.30 am P.T. under section officers. 9.30 – 12.30 Gun Drill I.A. + Musketry. 2 – 4 pm Packing Enfires, cleaning ammunition belts.	Initials
Khargpur	24/5/17		Cloudy weather, wind N to S.W. Programme of work:- 6.30 – 7.30 am Gun cleaning. 10.30 am } Company paraded full marching order, inspection of to 11 am } rifles, ammunition to 11.30 – 12.30 Issue of clothing. afternoon – Rest as per Orderly Orders.	Initials

Original
Army Form C. 2118.

WAR DIARY
or
INTELLIGENCE SUMMARY.

(Erase heading not required.)

Place	Date	Hour	Summary of Events and Information	Remarks and references to Appendices
Braypre	25/5/17		Fine weather. Brigade moved at 6.45 am under O.C. with transport. Equality paraded at full marching order, moved off at 7 am. 1st Half N. HAMCOURT. 2nd - N. TINCOURT. 3rd - N. end of NURLU. Arrived at EQUANCOURT at 2.15pm, the weather extremely oppressive & hot. No one fell out on the march. N. 1, 6 & > (Map Rf 57 c SE) Company bivouaced in their respective areas & dug & erected cover.	nil
Braype	26/5/17		Fine weather. Brigade arrived at 7 am. Company paraded at 9.30 am, rifles, ammunition and equipment, at 10.30 an inspection of feet. O.C. 1, No 3 + 4 Led officers left to carry out reconnaissance to new section	nil
Equan Court	27/5/17		Fine weather, wind bright air very hot. Company paraded at 9.30 am until 10.15 am. O.C. attended Church Parade. 2nd in Command visited 125 h.G.C. HQ at Leurry wood (Map Rf 57c SE: Q 1 & 2 3) Head Quarter staff arrived covers, map ps. No 1 Section Batt. EQUANCOURT at 2.30 pm received M.G.S. ends	nil

WAR DIARY or INTELLIGENCE SUMMARY

Army Form C. 2118.

Place	Date	Hour	Summary of Events and Information	Remarks and references to Appendices
Equancourt	27/5/17	6 a.m.	at QUEENS CROSS Q.28.d.2.7. relief completed at 5.30 am. No 2 section + 2 M.G's of No. 4 section moved to H.Q. Dessart Wood at 3 p.m. in reserve. No. 3 section + 2 guns No. 4 section left Equancourt at 6 p.m. for Dessart Wood. Moved forward to their respective M.G. positions at 8.30 p.m. No. 3 section relief completed at 11.30 p.m. — 4 " " " " " 1.9 a.m.	
Dessart Wood	28/5/17		Fine weather, bright sun, rain fell at 8.30 p.m. and S.W. The section in reserve were employed in digging latrines & keeping the camp in general order.— No. 1 section M.G. positions as under:- No. 1 gun at - Q.28. c. 2. 3 " 2 " " Q.28. c. 2. 3 A.A. gun " 3 " " Q.28. c. 6. 4 " 4 " " Q.28. c. 6. 5 A.A. gun Three new M.G. emplacements located at M.28.a.2.3 = W.28.c.4.8. No. 3 Section M.G. positions No. 1 " " Q.18. d. 3. 1 A.A. gun 3rd " " Q.18. c. 3. 3 Q.18. d. 4. 7 Q.18. c. 3. 1	

Original

Army Form C. 2118.

Instructions regarding War Diaries and Intelligence
Summaries are contained in F. S. Regs., Part II.
and the Staff Manual respectively. Title pages
will be prepared in manuscript.

WAR DIARY
or
INTELLIGENCE SUMMARY.
(Erase heading not required.)

Place	Date	Summary of Events and Information	Remarks and references to Appendices
Beau -(?) Mont	1 MAY 1917	No 4 section H.Q. position N° 1 Q.17.6.7.6. 2 Q.11.6.8.5. O.C. & 2nd i/c visited all H.Q. positions & number of enemy planes passed over our front line during the morning.	Nil
Beau mont	2/5/17	Weather cloudy. O.C. visited H.Q. positions 1,2,3. A.A. emplacement made at Q.23.a.4.3. The section in reserve was exercised in gun drill, I.A.T. mechanism, cleaning guns, ammunition.	Nil
Beau mont	3/5/17	Cloudy, rapid rate enemy by. Brigade General visited N°7 Gun H.Q. & the new A.A. M.G. Shell O.C. visited front line. Search located new H.Q. emplacement at R.7.c.8.9.9. R.7.c.1.8. R.12.a.1.8. the work of completion are commenced at these One gun of N° 4 Section was moved to the front line at 9.30 p.m.	Nil

Army Form C. 2118.

WAR DIARY
or
INTELLIGENCE SUMMARY.
(Erase heading not required.)

Place: **MAY 1917**

Hour	Summary of Events and Information	Remarks and references to Appendices
31/5/17	Fine bright am. Heavy S.W. the section. Heavy rain received from 6.30 to 7.30 am. PT. 7am. 7.30 am. Section drill and rifle M.G. Drill.	
	I.A. mechanism cleaning gun. pm. At the Coy H.Q. rendezvous Wood Q.28.a.3. the O.C. visited the intermediate line runway from R.13.b. citing to Q.17.b central locating new M.G. positions for the defence of the line. OC & 2nd in command visited M.G. positions in situation of strong point being established at QUEENS Cross Q.28.d.3.3. R.I. position at the following are— No 1 Q.28.d. 2.3 No 2 Q.28.d. 6.5 No 3 Q.29.c. 2.4 No 4 Q.29.c. 5.2 The section guns in reserve of No 4 section went into the front line. Relief sub-section officers at 9pm.	

L.J. Shuffrell Capt
O.C. 177 M.G.C.

Army Form C. 2118.

WAR DIARY
INTELLIGENCE SUMMARY.
(Erase heading not required.)

177 M.G. Coy

Place	Date	Hour	Summary of Events and Information	Remarks and references to Appendices
Gouzeaucourt Wood	1/6/17		Bright sun, very hot. OC waited the front line trenches, inspected the M.G. position & work being done at QUEENS CROSS £28 & 33. The section in reserve was exercised in M.G. gun drill & rifle exercises + I.A	
Gouzeaucourt Wood	2/6/17		Bright day & very hot. Section in reserve was exercised during the morning in P.T. M.G. Drill, gas helmets + I.A. All reserve belts we changed for wet belts. M.G. Position Target Range Am Exp Remarks R.7.3.9.7 R2.0.75 1,800' 1,200 Suspense enemy M.G. The enemy M.G. have been causing great annoyance to our working parties & & firing on anyone exposing any target, no more firing from enemy M.G. positions located by Capt. Stutfield were observed.	
Gouzeaucourt Wood	3/6/17		Bright sun very hot. The section in reserve was exercised in — 6.30 – 7.30 a.m. P.T. 9 – 10 a.m Gun rifle drill	

WAR DIARY
or
INTELLIGENCE SUMMARY.

Army Form C. 2118.

(Erase heading not required.)

Place	Date	Hour	Summary of Events and Information	Remarks and references to Appendices
Gonnezeured Wood	JUN 1917 3/6/17	10 – 10.30 a.m.	Boje reported 1 P/H Helmet drill resplendation.	
		10.45 – 12.30	Enemy aeroplane carried out a raid on enemy lines of communication, dropped five bombs. Enemy aircraft was observed about ½m from Q.18.c.9.3. Capt. Oldfield left for England.	OR
Gonnezeured Wood	4/6/17		Fine weather, very hot. Two officers of (200 MGC (6 in MGC) visited company HQ & MG positions at QUEEN'S CROSS Q.28.d.3.3. Took over the M.G. emplacements + relieved 172 R.O.E.C. Guns. 2nd in command visited the front, intermediate lines of trenches & inspected work of new emplacements being carried out.	OR
Gonnezeured Wood	5/6/17		Fine day. No 2 Section in reserve moved into the line relieved 4 guns of No 4 Section, relief completed at 11.30 p.m. 3 guns in Front line 1 gun in the intermediate line. No 1 Section sent a working party of 20 men to the front line.	

Original Secret

Army Form C. 2118.

WAR DIARY
or
INTELLIGENCE SUMMARY.
(Erase heading not required.)

No	Place	Date	Hour	Summary of Events and Information	Remarks and references to Appendices
	Gouzeaucourt Wood	5/9/17		Commenced work on the new M.G. positions located.	
	Gouzeaucourt Wood	6/9/17		Bright sunshine. 2 men commenced work on the new inspected M.G. positions being made. 2 gns of No1 system moved into the front line, occupying M.G. positions that had been made. Two guns of No 1 Section moved into the line took over gun positions:— No 5 Q.17.b.9.3 Intermediate line. 5 Q.12.a.8.3 Front line. The guns of No 2 Section occupying No 5 position at Q.17.b.9.3 moved to new gun position at Q.12.a.5.3, being relieved by guns of No 1 Section. Two temporary A.A. positions were made at Q.12.a.33 & Q.12.d.1.3. These positions were occupied by two guns of No1 Section firing down. No 2 gun Front line R.7.c.9.9 Range 2,080 + Enemy trenches marked. 3 — Q.12.d.7.2 2,000 — — — — — R.18d.9 & 2,600 — — — A.A. Gun Inter. 4,000 These guns fired on enemy in trenches from 5.15 pm. Artillery bombardment from 5.15 pm	

Army Form C. 2118.

WAR DIARY
or
INTELLIGENCE SUMMARY.
(Erase heading not required.)

Place	Date	Hour	Summary of Events and Information	Remarks and references to Appendices
Longueval	7/6/17		(Bright sun) very hot. 2. Command visited the front & intermediate line defences & arranged with Station officers to fire on enemy trenches & cross Roads. For the work done the M.G. positions were located & continued at: No 1 Q.18.b.6.5.0) in sunken Road leading to 2 Q.18.d.5.9) VILLERS PLOUICH 3 R.13.c.0.5 in C.T. The section in reserve were exercised as follows:- 6.30 – 7.30 am D.T. 9 – 10.30 Gun drill, mechanism, name drill 10.45 – 12.30 Aiming, gun ammunition, sticking open. Pte 50150 Henderson J wounded on road by fragment of shell 6pm at R.27.c.9.9	
Longueval	8/6/17		(Bright sun) 177 Brigadier Gen Pope Major & 2 in command visited the M.G. positions in front line trenches. Two new M.G. positions were located at 19.6.4.3. CT leading to outpost & Q.12.a.7.7 in forward plan of trenches.	

Original

Army Form C. 2118.

WAR DIARY
or
INTELLIGENCE SUMMARY.
(Erase heading not required.)

Place	Date	Hour	Summary of Events and Information	Remarks and references to Appendices
Gouy-en-Artois	8/6/17	Fine	MG Patrol Target Range. Ran Corp. Lewis L13.c.0.5. L31.c. to 27m + 1.50 Cross roads. Lt Anderson + 4 N.C.O.'s left for course of instruction on M.G. at Camiers. At 2 a.m. Gas alarm was sounded. All ranks turned out & paraded in front of Company HQ. On receipt of information from Brigade H.Q. that the alarm was false the men were dismissed at 2.15 am.	
Gouy-en-Artois	9/6/17		Cloudy, wind Showers. Capt. KING.C.R. arrived. 8 p.m. took over command of the Company. Work on M.G. positions rope continued during the night. 2nd in command visited the front line M.G. positions. M.G. moved forward to new position at Q.13.a.7.7.	
Gouy-en-Artois	10/6/17		Heavy rain accompanied by thunderstorm in the evening. 6.30 – 7.30 am, receipt of Company the parade at 9 a.m. – 10.30 am. L.i. drill Section Will will drill arms.	

Army Form C. 2118.

WAR DIARY
or
INTELLIGENCE SUMMARY
(Erase heading not required.)

Instructions regarding War Diaries and Intelligence Summaries are contained in F. S. Regs., Part II. and the Staff Manual respectively. Title pages will be prepared in manuscript.

Army Form C. 2118.

Place	Date	Hour	Summary of Events and Information	Remarks and references to Appendices
Inge[...]wood	12/6/17		Cont. 10.30–12.30 Gun team fired gusts at Q.28.a.17 100 yds range, rounds fired 500. In the afternoon O.C. & 2/Lt. Monks the M.G. positions in front Intermediate line. New emplacements located to opp. entrances to M.G. positions protecting the wire. Firg. Tgt. Rang. Rds. Exp. M.G. R.31.d.1.1. 2,800 2,000 R.13.c.0.4.	GHL
Inge[...]wood	11/6/17		Cloudy wind heavy rain during early morning. Evening the situation in [Kaasu?] carried on in relation [...] No. 46741 Pte. McFarland P. seriously wounded in [...] [...] died. Completing dug-outs & M.G. emplacements in front & Intermediate. Firing (by night) Tgt. Rang. Rds. Exp. Remarks M.G. Western 55–95 (Q.6.b.55 2,200→) 1,000 Removing Q.18.a. (Q.1.b.1.7 2,600→) 1,000 enemy dumps. 1 gun R.13.C.00.40 (L.31.C.0.4 2,600→) 1,000 1 gun (L.31.d. 2,500→) at Q.12.c.9.5. Alt. M.G. emplacement made at Q.12.c.9.5.	GHL

Original

Army Form C. 2118.

WAR DIARY
or
INTELLIGENCE SUMMARY.
(Erase heading not required)

Place	Date	Summary of Events and Information	Remarks and references to Appendices
Bouzincourt Wood	12/6/17	Weather somewhat cloudy, sunshine. 12 & 14 hours O.C. visited the front & reconfirmed line returned. Type of N° 3 & 4 guns, N° 4 to fire to the right, N° 3 to the left. The work in supplying M.G. position at R.7. c.5.1. was continued. Type of M.G. positions in front line for Coys. kept. T.S. 66. sheet 5.	G.R.K.
		N°1. Gun position R.7. b. u. 3. — firing right	
		„ 2. „ „ R.7. c. — „ right	
		„ 3. „ „ Q.12. b. 8.7. — „ left	
		„ 4. „ „ Q.12. b. 5.3. — „ left	
		„ 5. „ „ Q.12. a. 8.7. — „ left	
		A working party of 20 men were supposed to help in making approaches to M.G. positions at N° 1, & 4 & 5 positions also dugouts. Distribution of fatigue —	
		Front line 25 men (5 on gun position at trench Sq. R.13. a. 1. 7.	
		10 —	
		Lunéville line 25 men 5 on gun construction at trench Sq.	
		10 — N° 3 section at 11 pm	
		N° 4 section relieves N° 3 section at 11 pm	
Bouzincourt Wood	13/6/17	Bright sun moderate breeze. Men in reserve employed in cleaning guns equipment, collecting spare parts.	G.R.K.

Army Form C. 2118.

WAR DIARY
or
INTELLIGENCE SUMMARY.

(Erase heading not required.)

Date	Hour	Summary of Events and Information	Remarks and references to Appendices

Gouzeaucourt Wed. 13/6/17		Cont^d
		Work done
		at Q.18.b.8.4 a battle emplacement has been dug and O.T. Gun dug in to M.G. position. Dugouts trenches near the gun position were cleaned & improved
		
		Firing
		M.G.Barton Target Range Rds fired Remarks
		No1 Q.18.d. 55.95 R.28.a.9.7 2,700 2,000 1 x Road
		  " Q.18.d 60.95 R.23.c.3.3 2,600 2,000
		  R.27.c. 99 2,250 Enemy M.G.
		  R.15.c. 9.5 1,100 500 & Roads
		  Q.13. 8.8.7 R.1. 8.1.7 1,500
		
		No 2 #6.2.H.1 Pte McParland P. died of wounds at No. 34. C.C.S.
		buried at Red 62d A.9. 0.9.a central.
		
		Bright sun with fresh S.W. wind
		O.C. visited Brigade HQ.
		2nd in command reviews of F.G.C.M. at Leonard wood
		A working party of 16 men were employed on M.G. emplacements
		& preparing dug outs in the intermediate line.
		Night flares
		two battle emplacements (atop Lunn) at Q.18.a.7.5 & Q.18.a.8.5
		have been completed alongside pits for Gun teams. These
		two guns will be used for laying up flare on the S.O.S.
		line, many overhead wires fixed
		Firing Nil
			G.R.F.
			
			G.R.F.

Gouzeaucourt Thurs. 14/6/17			

Army Form C. 2118.

WAR DIARY
or
INTELLIGENCE SUMMARY.
(Erase heading not required.)

		Summary of Events and Information	Remarks and references to Appendices

Gouy-en-Artois 14/6/17

The enemy shelled our front line with small shells & M.G. was also with.
At 8.15 am at Q.18.d.3.3 an enemy shell fell on dugout occupied by Lewis Gunners.
Killing Nº 57385 Pte HINMAN T.
85/48 " PRITCHARD A
Wounding 16607 " LACEY J.
Pte Hinman + Pritchard A. buried at Q.27.a.2.3

Gouzeaucourt 15/6/17

Bright sun very hot.
The section to reserve were reviewed at
6.30 to 7.30 am   P.T.
9 10.30 "   Gun drill + lecture
10.30 11 a.m lecture - flyers to finds
11.   12.30 "   musketry rally drill
OC visited intensively two Companies in the trenches. M.G. officer had arranged to output M.G. fire. Having dispositions of M.G. in different companies that took over and their dogs in trenches.
M.G. protecting M.G. emplacements reviewing reports. Having had firing kit.
Enemy M.Gs active on our left front.

WAR DIARY or INTELLIGENCE SUMMARY

Army Form C. 2118.

Place: Souchez N/ Wood
Date: 16/6/17

Very hot with bright sun. Wind dangerous.
O.C. 175 Coy Rejoined the trophés until O.C. 177 Coy inspected M.G. Positions in intermediate line.
Night done.

Barrage by M.G. employments covering 3,000. All sets being shot through have been covered with either frog a raid was carried out by the Lincoln Regt covering 3 officer + 60 OR. It was arranged for 10 M.G. to lay down a M.G Barrage in case of counter attack.
A M.G Barrage was called for at 12:45 a.m. immediately opened fire many overhead indirect fires changing the following points to enemy trenches:-

Gun Position	Target	Range	Gun Emp	Remarks
No 1	Q.18.d.57.95	Barrage	1,950*	2,000	Gun firing from 12:45 a.m
2	Q.18.d.60.95	between	2,050	1,500	to 1:10 a.m.
3	Q.18.a.95.60	R.19.7.4 +	1,500	1,500	
4	Q.18.c.6.9.	R.19.8.7.	2,150	1,000	
5	Q.18.a.50.00		2,300	1,250	
6	Q.18.a.4.7.		2,000	1,250	
7	Q.18.a.2.7.	R.19.a.6.4.5.	1,950	1,250	
8	Q.18.b.40.25	R.19.c.85.15.	2,500	1,350	an enemy M.G. was
9	Q.18.b.30.25	R.19.c.30.75 +	2,000	1,250	Silenced by own M.G
10	Q.18.b.25.25	R.19.c.9.5.4.3.		750	fire
		R.19.7.3	2,000		
			13,100		

Heavy firing on Trenches were noted from Headquarters to

WAR DIARY
or
INTELLIGENCE SUMMARY

Army Form C. 2118.

(Erase heading not required.)

Place	Date	Hour	Summary of Events and Information	Remarks and references to Appendices
Gouzeaucourt Wood	16/6/17		Contd. E.g. M.G. gun positions. The raid carried out every evening. Prisoner was taken from pillbox, firing very successful.	
Gouzeaucourt Wood	17/6/17		Bright sun, very hot wind, mild sunset. O.C. visited the front line with 2nd i/c of 175th Coy. The section in reserve was examined. from 6.30 to 7.30 9.T 9 " 11.30 9.T 11.30 " 1.30 sleeping gun frontage rivet filling 1.30 " 3.30 Section died with arms. Work Done. Glengarrie implements have been sandbagged. Dugout at Q.18.d.4.3 two guns made to replace on damaged revisited parapets sandbagged. Dugout to M.G. position also dugout night firing sticks painted with luminous paint has been put up at each M.G. position allotted own front line during the night.	
Gouzeaucourt Wood	18/6/17		Fine weather, wind showers. The section in reserve finished at 6.15 a.m. 6.30 7.30 cleaning camp, hygiene, diens 9 " 12 Gun drill, musketry, wind letters in right 12. Turning Donn, covering cops to M.G. positions in the front line.	

Army Form C. 2118.

Original

WAR DIARY
or
INTELLIGENCE SUMMARY

(Erase heading not required.)

Place	Date	Hour	Summary of Events and Information	Remarks and references to Appendices
Gonnecourt Wood	18/6/17		Gorta + Intermediate line. High Firing Target.	
			Sup. pos. Target Range L.a.a. Bsps	
			① R /3.c.5.5. L37.d.1.1. 2750× 1,250 |{1× Roads rapport enemy	EPK
			② Q7.a. 6.8. R3.a.2.7 2000× 500 M.G	
			③ Q7.c. 8.9. L31.d.2.9 2000× 300 Railway	
			④ Q18.d.5.95. R1.b.1.8 2550 1500 × Roads used by enemy.	
			Enemy M.Gs were active during the night.	
			High ex. heavy shower of rain fell responsed by thunderstorm	
			Her Gw. reserve were employed on —	
			P.T. 6.30 to 7.30	
			Gun drill + 9.30 – 12.30	
			Work done	
			Four dugouts completed at Coy H.Q.	
			No 1 Ammunition repair shop	
			— 2. 20ft dug down for men in reserve	
			3 care for reserve L.a.a. to	
			4 Magazines	
Gonnecourt Wood	19/6/17		The lection in trenches were employed on sandbagging + draining M.G. supp trenches. Trenches in very wet muddy	GRK
			condition. Target Range S.a. Bsps	
			Q18.d.5.95. R1.6. 1.6. 550 1500 Cross Roads	

Original

WAR DIARY or INTELLIGENCE SUMMARY

Army Form C. 2118.

(Erase heading not required.)

7 M.G. Coy.

Place	Date	Hour	Summary of Events and Information	Remarks and references to Appendices
Gouzeaucourt Wood	19/6/17		A reconnaissance was made of the forward line of outposts with a view of locating M.G. positions. The following sites were chosen as approximate. Batch pos:– No 1. R.7.b.36. No 3. Q.12.b.96. No.4. Q.6.d.4.1. No.2. R.7.a.5.5. No.5. Q.6.c.7.1.	G.R.K.
1 Gouzeaucourt Wood	20/6/17		Heavy showers during the morning with bright sun at intervals, no work done. Men in reserve. A working party was sent to help in construction of new transport lines at P.13.5.d. Cent., the remainder received letters. Enemy by compass traversing shell 9-10.30 am from Quest Tilloy. 10.30-12.0 noon Enemy at night by our army fort. 10.30-11.30 p.m. (The targets who dodged after guns were laid the targets was reported by electric torch, results obtained were good.) work done:– framing of trench sandbagging of M.G. positions. four telephony M.G. positions made in the forward line of outposts. Night firing target range No Coy. position Q.18.a.55.95 R.18.b.1.8. 2,550 x 1,500 Rounds.	G.R.K.
Gouzeaucourt Wood	26/6/17		Fresh wind with heavy showers of rain. O.C. & 2nd Lt. G. of 175 M.G. Coy. visited the trenches & inspected	G.R.K.

Army Form C. 2118.

WAR DIARY
or
INTELLIGENCE SUMMARY
(Erase heading not required.)

Place	Date	Hour	Summary of Events and Information	Remarks and references to Appendices
Gouzeaucourt Wood	26/6/17	6 p.m.	D.G. position. The trenches were very muddy. The section in reserve supplied a working party of 1 N.C.O. + 8 men to help in construction of new trapboard line. 1 N.C.O. + 4 men reported to O.C. 256 Tunnelling Coy R.E. for a 2 weeks course of instruction in making small dugouts. Work done. Cleaning + training of trench T.M. & position. The construction of M.G. position in the forward line of outposts was carried out + covered stations for the gun were commenced.

Gun No. Target. Range.
① R.7. d.6.8. Rg.4.6.8. 2,400 x
② Q16.d.59.95. JR8.6.15.b.{2,000/2,500}{1,000/200}
    J2.6.3.4 2,500
D.T. — 6.30 to 7.30 a.m.
9 — 9.30
9.30 — 10.30 — care & use of box respirator
10.30 — 11 Aim, Trigger & firing + care of Lewis gun
11.0 to 12.30 practical instruction in making small dugouts | C.S.K. |
| Gouzeaucourt Wood | 27/6/17 | | Heavy rain during the morning. No instruction in trenches was observed. Enemy working party of 6 men observed Road used by enemy when Lewis gun fire was used. Artillery observation in enemy trenches | G.S.K. |

Army Form C. 2118.

WAR DIARY
or
INTELLIGENCE SUMMARY.

(Erase heading not required.)

Place	Date	Summary of Events and Information	Remarks and references to Appendices
Gouzeaucourt Wood	22/6/17	Coys. Work done. Cleaning, thinning tracks & preparing & M.G. position. The 4 M.G. posted in forward line of thinkers were entirely material carried forward for construction of shelters for Lewis Teams. At 11.30 p.m. the company was relieved by 17th H.L.I. The relief was carried out satisfactorily the company was marched to rest camp at Equancourt. W 16 d. 59	A
Equancourt	23/6/17	Few light showers of rain in the morning. The company paraded at 9 am 9 – 11 at Cleaning guns, Ammunition to 11 – 12.30 washing & Rubentoring the camp.	A
Equancourt	24/6/17	Company paraded at 9.30 am under O C attended Church Parade.	A
Equancourt	25/6/17	Company on rest, the following programme of work was carried out. 6.30 to 7.30 am PT 9 – 10 Inspection of rifles, numerals. 10 – 11 Cleaning Guns. 11 – 12 Cleaning pans pads, reading timber.	A

WAR DIARY
or
INTELLIGENCE SUMMARY

Army Form C. 2118.

Date	Hour	Summary of Events and Information	Remarks and references to Appendices
Equancourt 26/6/17		The following programme of work was carried out:-	
	6.30 – 7.30	P.T.	
	9 – 10	Gun drill with auxiliary mounting	
	10 – 11	Lecture "Stoppage Tives" (for Lewis Machine Gunners)	
		Mechanism (for attached men)	
	11 – 12	Stripping	
	12 – 1	S.A.	E.R.K.
Equancourt 27/6/17		The following were carried out as follows:-	
	6.30 – 7.30	P.T.	
	9 – 10	S.A. (for Lewis Machine Gunners)	
		Mechanism (for attached men)	
	10 – 11	Practice in use of drill (for Lewis Gunners)	
		Gun drill for attached men.	
	11 – 12	Points B.D.v S.A. } for attached men.	
	12 – 1 pm		
	1 –	Inspect auxiliary fire practical demonstration (for Lewis Machine Gunners)	O.R.K.
Equancourt 28/6/17		Heavy thunderstorm in the evening. The following was carried out as follows:-	
	6.30 – 7.30	P.T.	
	9 – 1 pm	Firing on Range	E.R.K.

Army Form C. 2118.

WAR DIARY
or
INTELLIGENCE SUMMARY
(Erase heading not required.)

Place	Date	Hour	Summary of Events and Information	Remarks and references to Appendices
Equancourt	29/6/17		Fine warm. The following programme of work was carried out:—	
		6.30 – 7.30	P.T.	
		9 – 10	Regtl. light fixing	
		10 – 11	Section drill	
		11 – 12	Lecture: Hygiene discipline	
		12 – 1pm	Care + use of box respirators & P.H. Helmets.	E.R.K.
Equancourt	30/6/17		Dull misty morning.	
		6.30 – 7.30 am	P.T.	
		9.30 –	Heavy showers of rain prevented further training being carried out. Lieut L.A. MILLETT M.C. left at 6.0 am for R.G. Course at Camiers.	E.R.K.

E.R. Huey. Capt.
O.C. No. 177 M.G. Coy.

Army Form C. 2118.

WAR DIARY
or
INTELLIGENCE SUMMARY
(Erase heading not required.)

177 M.G. Coy

Vol 6

Place	Date	Hour	Summary of Events and Information	Remarks and references to Appendices
Equancourt	1/7/17		Dull day - some rain. Company paraded at 8.15am for preparing timbers in preparation for move. Company moved camp from V.16.d.8.9 to north of FINS V.6.a.0.9 (Map 57cSE).	
V.6.a.0.9	2/7/17		Began erection of semi-permanent building. Fine warm day. Programme of work:— 6.30 - 7.30 P.T. 9 - 10 I.A. 10 - 11 Foot Drill 11 - 12 Battle Issues for Guns 12 - 1pm Gun Drill (Cleaning mounting) 2.30 - 4.30 Cleaning Limbers 6.30 - 7.30 P.T. 9 - 10 Rifle exer 10 - 11 Gun Drill 11 - 12 S.A. 12 - 1pm Lectures, Observation etc 2.30 - 4.30 Cleaning limbers Continuing of semi-permanent structures. The above programme of work was carried out.	

WAR DIARY or INTELLIGENCE SUMMARY

Army Form C. 2118.

Original   Secret

Place	Date	Hour	Summary of Events and Information	Remarks and references to Appendices
16.a.0.9.	3/7/17		Bull - coin run Programme of work 6.30 – 7.30 PT Trained her 9-10 Rifles (müder fire) 10-11 LA 11-12 Rapid Loading 12-1 Bur drill (lower portion) The above programme was carried out	Attached hw. 9-10 Triangle of Error te. 10-11 LA 11-12 Point B.O. 12-1 exercise in recognition of targets
16.a.0.9	4/7/17		Tone bud drill. Programme of work 6.30 to 7.30 PT Trained her 9-10 LA 10-11 Explanation of Compass & its uses 11-12 Lewis gun (Instructs repair test) 12-1 Return to quarters Above programme was carried out	Attached hw. 9-10 Judging 10-11 distance 11-12 LA Rapid filling by hand 12-1 Gas Parts shown & explained

WAR DIARY or INTELLIGENCE SUMMARY

Army Form C. 2118.

Place	Date	Hour	Summary of Events and Information	Remarks and references to Appendices
V6a09	5/7/17		Fine sunny day. Programme of work 6.30 to 7.30 a.m. Immed. + attacked hrs. 9 - 1 pm Construction of M.G. emplacements, dugouts + revetting. Above programme was carried out	
V6a09	6/7/17		Fine sunny day. Programme of work 6.30 - 7.30 Immed hrs 9-10 10-11 Lewis gun drill (practical work) 11-12 Photo or Lewis gun 12-1 Contents of Lewis gun spare parts box, stoppages & their immediate remedies. Above programme was carried out. Fine but dull. Programme of work. Lewis gun drill 9-10 9-10 Lewis gun drill 10-11 Lewis gun drill 11-12 Gun cleaning & gun 12-1 Do.	
V6a09	7/7/17			

WAR DIARY or INTELLIGENCE SUMMARY

Army Form C. 2118.

Place	Date	Summary of Events and Information	Remarks and references to Appendices
V6 a 0 9	2/7/17	Cora 10 - 11 PA 11 - 12 Artillery hunting drill 12 - 1 Care & cleaning of guns Attended by 9.30 LP 10 - 11 Gun drill 11 - 12 Practice in use of dial 12 - 1 stripping above programme was carried out.	
		Dull day - rain Church Parade 10 am Roman Catholic 10.30 C of E 9 am RC	
V6 a 0 9	8/7/17	Company busied in these parades having camp at 2.30 p.m Fine but dull - rain in evening 	
V6 a 0 9	9/7/17	Company paraded for fatigues in preparation for move. No 3 Section paraded at 9.15 a.m with working order, marched off 9.30 am in train for VILLERS CARBONNEL for duty at Heath Dump NO Limbers moved off at 10.30 am	

Army Form C. 2118.

WAR DIARY
or
INTELLIGENCE SUMMARY.

(Erase heading not required.)

Place	Date	Hour	Summary of Events and Information	Remarks and references to Appendices
V6a09	9/7/17		Fine hot but dull. Company paraded for fatigue - cleaning camp - packing leather. The Company paraded at 11.30 am & marched off at 12 noon to new camp at O.16 Central near Caestre arriving 3 pm	
V6a09	10/7/17		Fine sunny day. Parades 6.30. 7.30. Clean fatigue 9 am. Clean fatigues	
V6a09	11/7/17		Fine sunny day. Programme of work as stated below. 6.45 – 7.45 am Company Drill 9 – 10 Gun Drill 10 – 11 Stripping 11 – 12 Between trades training 2.30 – 3.30 am Revolver Shooting 6.45 – 7.45 am Company Drill 9 – 10 Gun Drill 10 – 11 Stripping 11 – 12 " 7.30 – 3.30 Revolver Shooting. The above programme was carried out.	

(A7292). Wt. W12839/M1293. 75,000. 1/17. D. D. & L., Ltd. Forms/C.2118/14.

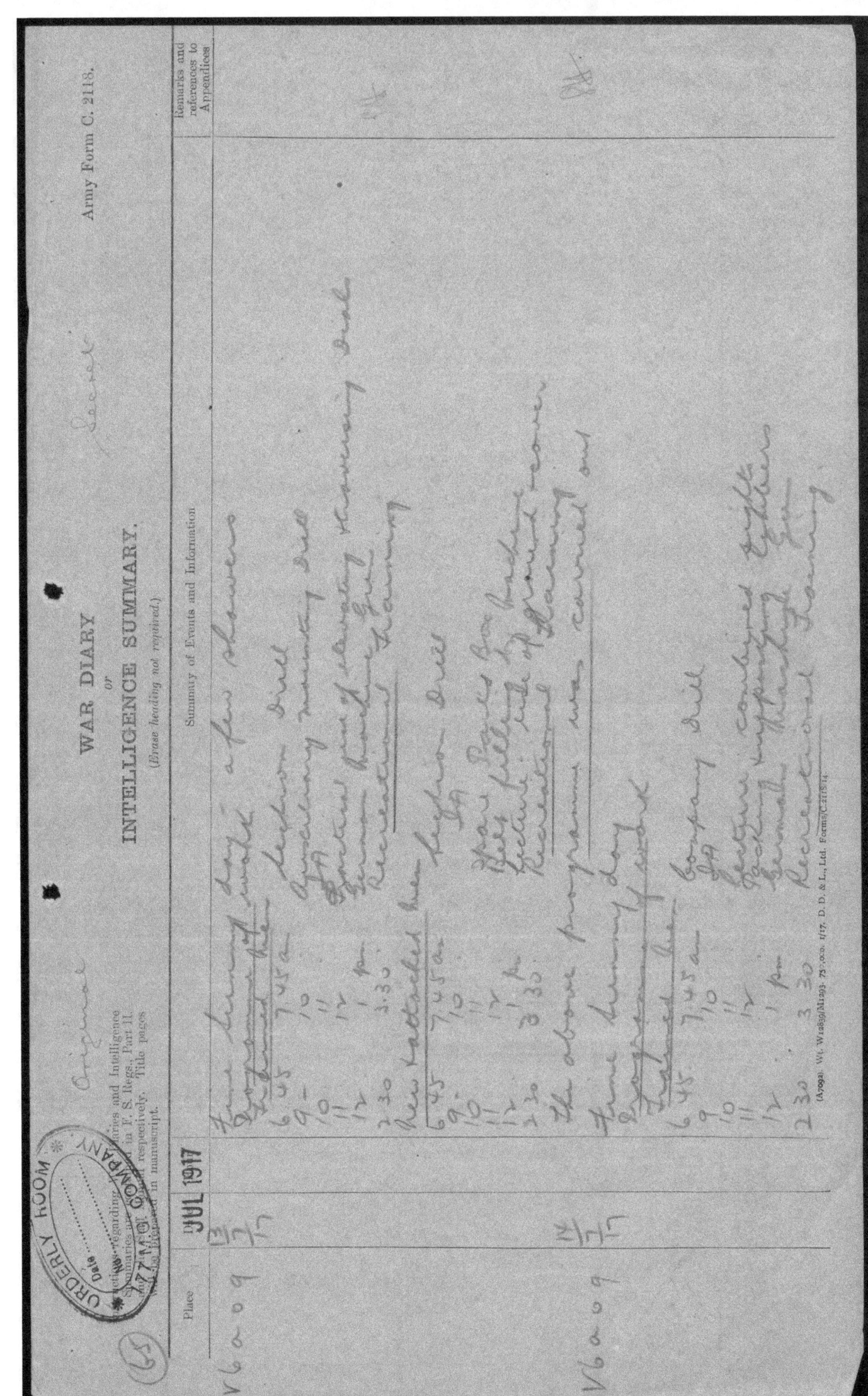

Army Form C. 2118.

WAR DIARY
or
INTELLIGENCE SUMMARY.

(Erase heading not required.)

Original   Secret

Place	Date	Hour	Summary of Events and Information	Remarks and references to Appendices
VI a 0 9	14/7/17		Scott New Battalion Hrs 6.45. 7.45. Company Drill 9 - 10 " 10 - 11 " 11 - 12 Bonnie BDR 1 - 1.30 Revision of Musketry 2.30 3.30 Recruits Training Above programme was carried out Fine weather - sultry - rain in evening. Church Parade RC 9 am CE 10.30. Wes l 10.0.	ott
VI a 0 9	15/7/17			
VI a 0 9	16/7/17		Changeable weather - permits grain followed by bright sunshine. Programme of Work 6.45 7.45 Section Drill 9 - 10 " German bathes fm 10 - 11 " bathing in recovering 11 - 12 OA1	ott

Army Form C. 2118.

Original   Secret

WAR DIARY
or
INTELLIGENCE SUMMARY
(Erase heading not required.)

Place	Date	Hour	Summary of Events and Information	Remarks and references to Appendices
V6a09	16/7/17		Coat	
		12-1	Lectures indirect fire	
		2.30-3.30	Recreational training	
			New entrenched tool	
		6.45-7.45am	Extension drill	
		9-10	Lewis & Hotchkiss gun	
		11-11	stripping	
		11-12	gas	
		12-1pm	Lewis instructional	
		2.30-3.30	Range work	
			above programme was carried out.	
V6a09	17/7/F		Changeable weather - periods of rain followed by bright sunshine.	ft
			Programme of work framed was retained viz.	
		6.45-7.45	Company drill	
		9-10	}	
		10-11	} Construction of H.G. emplacements, dugouts &	
		11-12	}	
		12-1	}	
		2.30-3.30	Recreational training	
			above programme was carried out	

Army Form C. 2118.

WAR DIARY
or
INTELLIGENCE SUMMARY
(Erase heading not required.)

Original   Seaca

Place	Date	Hour	Summary of Events and Information	Remarks and references to Appendices
V6a o.9	18/7/17		Changed weather. 6.45 to 7.45 Company Drill Lecture hut 9-10 Lecture in Gas in Trench warfare 10-11 S.A. (Bayonet) 11-12 Gunshot Rifle 12-1 Lecture Military Hygiene New Battalion hut 9-10 S.A. 10-11 Lecture- Overhead fire 11-12 Guarding Country Drill 12-1 Lecture Military Hygiene 2.30-3.30 Recreational Training Above programme was carried out Fine sunny day	
V6a o.9	19/7/17		6.45 to 7.45 Company Drill Lecture hut 8.45 am Enemy Range (Firing from ambuscade mounting) now attached here 9-10 S.A. 10-11 Practice in use of duck 11-12	H

Original   Secret   Army Form C. 2118.

WAR DIARY
or
INTELLIGENCE SUMMARY
(Erase heading not required.)

69 77 M.G.C.

Place	Date	Summary of Events and Information	Remarks and references to Appendices
Vba09	19/7/17	12-1 Notes on Reconnaissance 2.30 - 3.30 Recreational Training Above programme of work was carried out.	M
Vba09	20/7/17	Fine sunny day 6.45 - 7.45 Company lecture drill, Bayonet Fighting Trained by: 9-10 Gun drill (two mountings) 10-11 Cleaning spare parts 11-1 Bayonet training Men attached her 9-10 Gun drill (two mountings) 10-11 ――― 11-12 Lecture. Compound sights 12-1 Grenade Training 2.30 - 3.30 Recreational Training Above programme of work was carried out.	
Vba09	21/7/17	Fine sunny day 6.45 - 7.45 Company lecture drill Trained her 9-10 Lecture:- h.Q. its duties 10-11 Notes on field work	M

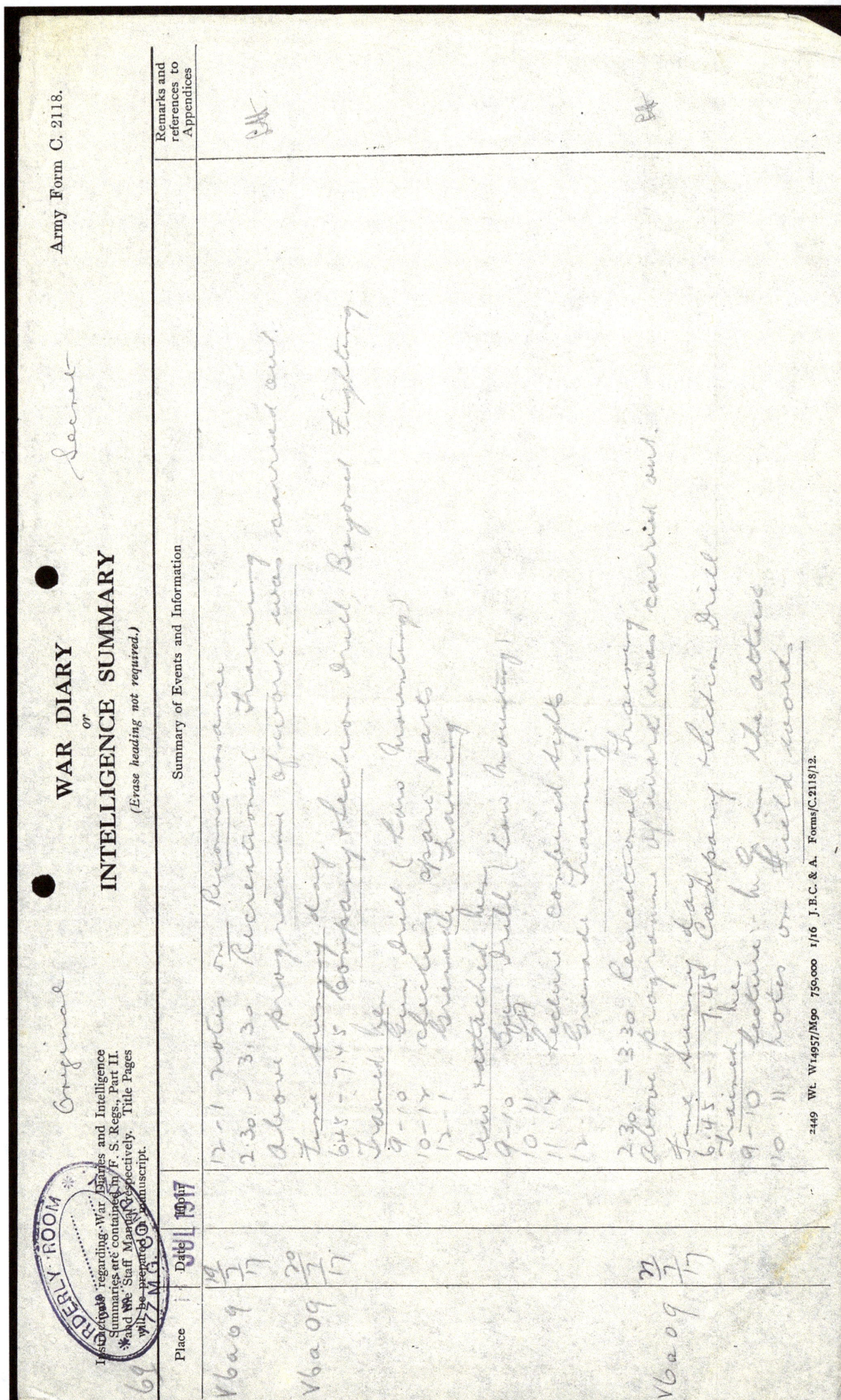

Army Form C. 2118.

Original   Issue

WAR DIARY
or
INTELLIGENCE SUMMARY.
(Erase heading not required.)

Place	Date	Hour	Summary of Events and Information	Remarks and references to Appendices
V6a09	2/7/17		Men attached here	
		9-10	Captains of Shaftsbury's horses	
		10.11	Picture	
		11am	cleaned tuif/kitbag for swimming sports	
V6a09	22/7/17		Fine Sunny day	
			Church Parade	
		10a	C of E	
		9 30	Non C of E	
		9 a	R.C.	
V6a09	23/7/17		Fine Sunny day	
			Parade	
		6.45-7.45	Company Section drill	
			Company No 2 Section practising sports for Brigade	
			Section Braeries	
			No 2 Section paraded for about 9.15 am	
			Coys Operation orders by Capt Elling enclosed und	
			Coys Diary	
			These operation were carried out	
			Company returned on return from operations	
V6a09	24/7/17		Fine sunny day	
			Parade	
		6.45-7.45	Company Section drill	

WAR DIARY or INTELLIGENCE SUMMARY

Army Form C. 2118.

Original   Secret

Place	Date	Hour	Summary of Events and Information	Remarks and references to Appendices
V6a09	24/7/17		Gents	
			Issued Kgs	
		9.10	SA	
		10.11		
		11.12		
		12.1	Lectrie Machine Guns in attack	
			Rev. moveda ha	
		9.10	SA	
		10.12		
		12.1	Going of ground ranges for sungs	
		2.30-3.30	Lective Lewis Gunng (proposed to stop 6th)	
			deposit of test ray planes were carried out	
			the above	
V6a09	25/7/17		dull day some showers	
			parade 7.45 - 7.45am Company drill	
			Issued his Bren MG (LP)	
		9.10		
		10.11	Lectures a Regimental	
		11.12	German Machine Gunng	
		12.1	General Training	

WAR DIARY
or
INTELLIGENCE SUMMARY
(Erase heading not required.)

Army Form C. 2118.

Place	Date	Hour	Summary of Events and Information	Remarks and references to Appendices
V6a09	25/7/17		Enemy attacked by 9 – 10 10 – 11 use of mouth ?? gas shell 12 – 1 dropping shrapnel 2.30 to 3.30 Recreational training	A
V6a09	26/7/17		Heavy enemy day programme. Have Company Drill 16.45 – 17.45 Company Drill Enemy attacked his ? – ? Station occupation of ??? (Booking Communic- ammunition supply ??? Above programme of work was carried on ?? heavy day ?????? Tactical Exercise & attacked operator order by Capt S??????	A
V6a09	27/7/17			
V6a09	28/7/17		Cpl ????? reported from course of L.G instruction at ????? M.G Rich reported from M.G reinforcement ????	A

WAR DIARY
or
INTELLIGENCE SUMMARY
(Erase heading not required.)

Army Form C. 2118.

Place	Date	Summary of Events and Information	Remarks and references to Appendices
V6a o 9	26/7/17	Division tactical Exercise repeated as on 27th	
V6a o 9	27/7/17	Heavy thunderstorm in morning accompanied by torrential rain / showers throughout the day. Church Parade (C of E) 11.45 a RC 8.30 — Nonconformist 9.30 —	hilly
V6a o 9	29/7/17	Weather dry with heavy cloud. Few light showers in the evening. Company paraded at 8.0 am for Range firing at N.16 & (Irvington) + N 16 at 4.5. 50 (lucks)	hilly
V6a o 9	31/7/17	Fine weather with little sunshine. Showers in the afternoon. Evening. Programme of training. Company Drill 7.45 to 8.15 Sand bag — 8.30 — 9.0 in attack 9 – 10 " bats or field work 10 – 11 " " " " 11.0 vaccinated them 9.0 " " Practice on use of sub expired caused 10 " Indication 5 – 6 pm Recreational Training	hello

O.O. No. 1777 M.G. Coy.

Secret.   Original   Copy No. 13

Operation Order No. 1.
by Capt. G. R. King
Commdg 177 Machine Gun Coy
23-7-17

Map Ref 57c S.W.

The 177 Infty Brigade will carry out a Tactical exercise on July 23/1917, when they will attack the enemy trenches between O.21.b.70.75. & O.22.a.4.4. X Brigade will attack on the left & Y Brigade on the right, at the same time the 2/4 Leicester Regt. will be in support 2/5 Leicester Regt. in reserve.

Objectives
(a) Sunken Road from
O.21. b. 70. 75.
to O.22. a. 4. 4.
(b) German Trench running through
O.21. b. 6. 8 and
O.22. a. 0. 0
Each position will be consolidated when captured.

177 Machine Gun Coy
(a) O.C. No. 2 Section will detail two guns to each assaulting Battalion. These guns will act under the orders of each Battalion Commander and will report at respective Battalion parade grounds at 9.15 am
(b) O.C. No 3 section will remain in present positions in our front line from where they will not move without orders from the G.O.C.
These guns will cover Infty from Counter attack especially from their flanks.

(c) OC No 4 Section will be in position at assembly Trench "b" by zero minus 30 minutes, will move forward, as soon as second objective is taken, to the first objective and consolidation.

(d) OC No. 1. Section will be in reserve in trenches at O.16.c.6.5.

Dress 5 Fighting Order

Carrying Parties 6 Arrangements will be made for carrying parties, will be detailed to sections.

Dumps 7 Main dumps, Company H.Q. at O.16.c.4.5
for { Ammunition
      { Rations
      { Water
Forward dumps at O.16.c.0.2. & O.22.a.3.9
Section Officers will be responsible that men know exact position of these dumps

Ammunition Supply 8 Section Officers will be responsible that on reaching final objective further ammunition dumps will be organised, that the chain of ammunition supply is in perfect working order. A responsible N.C.O. will be detailed for this task.
Positions of new dumps will be forwarded to Company H.Q.
R.E. Material tools will be drawn from Battalion dumps by arrangement with C.O.

Communication 9 Communication will be maintained between Company H.Q. & Nos 2, 3 & 4 sections by using Battalion telephone to Brigade H.Q.

Each section will also arrange a system of runners in case of breakdown of telephonic communication.

Position of H.Qs
10. Advanced Brigade H.Q will be at O.16.c.4.6.
Battalion HQ of the assaulting Battalions will be O.16.c.1.2. & O.22.a.25.90.
177 Machine Gun Coy HQ will be at O.16.c.5.6.
Positions of R.A.Ps will be at O.16.c.2.2 & O.22.a.5.9.

Zero Hour
11. Zero hour will be at 11 a.m. A state of war will exist from Zero minus 10 minutes.

12. Acknowledge.

Issued by D.R.L.S. at
Copy No 1 Brigade HQ
       2 OC 7/4 Lines
       3 "   7/5
       4 "   7/4 Leics
       5 "   7/5
       6 "   177 Lt. T.M.B
       7 "   No 1 Section
       8 "   2
       9 "   3
      10 "   4
      11 Transport Officer
      12 War Diary
      13 War Diary
      14 Files

Original   Copy No 13

Operation Order No 2.   26.7.17.
by Capt. G. K. King
commdg 177 Machine Gun Coy

Map reference 57c S.W.
and 177 Infty Brigade trench map

1. Information. On July 27. 1917 the 59th Division will attack the enemy trenches between M.1.b.70.20. and M.36.d.40.20.
At the same time the 11th Division will attack on the right and the 11th Division on the left of the 59th Division.
The attack of the 59th Division will be made by the 178th Infty Brigade on the right and the 177 Infty Brigade on the left.

2. Objectives. The objectives of these Brigades are
    a. The GERMAN front line trench.
    b. STAR TRENCH and MOON TRENCH.
    c. TREACLE TRENCH.
Each objective when captured will be consolidated.
After the capture of TREACLE TRENCH the 176 Infty Brigade will pass through 178 and 177 Infty Brigade and will consolidate a position in continuation of PROMETHEOS TRENCH and WINDMILL MOUND.
The attack of the 177 Infty Brigade will be made by the 2/4 Lincoln Regt on the right and the 2/5 Lincoln Regt on the left. 2/4 Leicester Regt will be in support and will form up behind 2/5 Lincoln Regt.

...[illegible] will be in reserve behind X[?]
Redoubt Left.

3. M.G. a. C.O. No 2 [?] section will attach two guns
Sim. Coy. to each assaulting Battalion. They will not
be under the orders of O.C. Battalions and
will be used for the consolidation of
TRENCHES TRENCH.

b. O.C. No 3. Section will remain in our
front line and after capture of third objective
they will act as reserve.

c. O.C. No 6 section will make all
arrangements and necessary calculations to
bring fire to bear on [illegible] COMMUNICATION
TRENCH.

d. O.C. No 1 section will make all
arrangements and necessary calculations
to bring fire to bear on MARS COMMUNICA-
TION TRENCH.

e. O.C. No 4 section will place his
guns between points J.6.c.y.4 and J.6.c.05.05.
f. O.C. No 1 section will place his guns
at points J.6.b.7.6, J.6.b.8.7, J.6.b.b.4,
and J.6.b.0.2. Both sections will fire
at zero plus 11 minutes in accordance
with Artillery Barrage and prepare to
move forward in order immediately third
objective is captured.
No 4 section to MOON TRENCH.

4. Communications. Communication will be maintained
between Company H.Qand Nos 1 section by
using Battalion telephone to Brigade H.Q.

4. ... setting up a breakdown of system of
runners will be arranged for beforehand
between [...] between Company HQ and Bn.

5. Two delivery Telephone between HQ & Bn
sections cannot [...] to consolidate
and are in position arrangements must
be made for a system of runners beforehand.

5. Carrying Arrangements will be made for carrying
   Parties   parties and will be detailed to sections.

6. Ammunition Section Officers will be responsible that
   Supply   on reaching the final position further
              ammunition dumps are organised at
              once, and that a continuous chain of
              ammunition is established. An Officer
              will be detailed for this work.
              Positions of new dumps N.P. and
              dumps will be forwarded to Company
              HQ. R.E. Material & Tools will be
              drawn from Battalion dumps by
              arrangement with Commanding
              Officers.

7. Dumps   Main dump J.6.b.30.25 for
                                   } Ammunition
                                     Rations
                                     Water
            Forward dumps at J.6.b.38. and
            J.6.b.94.

8. Positions [Brigade] and Company HQ will be
   of HQs   at J.6.b.30.15.

"Battalion H.Q. of assaulting battn.
will be at 36.b.c.2.9 & 36.b.6.55 on."

9. Reg Aid Posts   36.b.2.9, 36.b.6.55.

10. Situation   To Company HQ frequently.
    Reports

11. Synchron-   O.C. No 2 section will see that Brigade
    isation of   H.Q. on his way out not later than 6/15 a.m.
    Watches

12. Zero   Zero hour will be at 9 a.m.
    hour

13. Flares   Flares will be lit by advanced line
                   at zero plus 30 minutes.

14. Acknowledge

................E.R. King............... Capt.
O.C, No. 177 M.G. Coy.

Issued by 2nd O.C. List
Copy No 1 Brigade HQ
       2 O.C.   1/4 Lincoln
       3   1/5
       4   1/4 Leicester
       5   1/5
       6   177 L.T.M.B.
                 .... Section
       7   2
       8   3
       9   4
       10
       11 Transport Officer
       12 War Diary
       13
       14 File

WAR DIARY or INTELLIGENCE SUMMARY

Army Form C. 2118.

Vol 7 (original)

Place	Date	Hour	Summary of Events and Information	Remarks and references to Appendices
016a09	1/8/17		Havent. Programme of training 6.45 - 7.45 a.m. Company Section drill	
			Tapped hin	
		9.10	D.A Lewis attacked him	
		10.11	Rapier equipment 9.10 Rifles covered rgts	
		11.12	L.O.S.T 10.11 D.A 11.12 Contests of gas masks & box, first aid case practice	
		2.3 pm	Reverend Training	
016a09	2/8/17		Raining. Company backed for Programme of work	
			Company backed from 6.15 to 8.0 am	
			Programme of work	
		9.10	Extn Ladies Guns in open warfare	St
		10.11	" " " " "	
		11.12	Machine guns in open warfare (advancing toemping view position)	
		2-3 pm	Reverend Training	
016a09	3/8/17		Programme of work	
		6.45-7.45	Company Section drill	
		9-12	Machine guns in open warfare (advancing, air water ammunition supply)	
		2-3	Communication, rigging training	
			Reverend	
			Officer 9/17 relieving thing R.E. explement	St

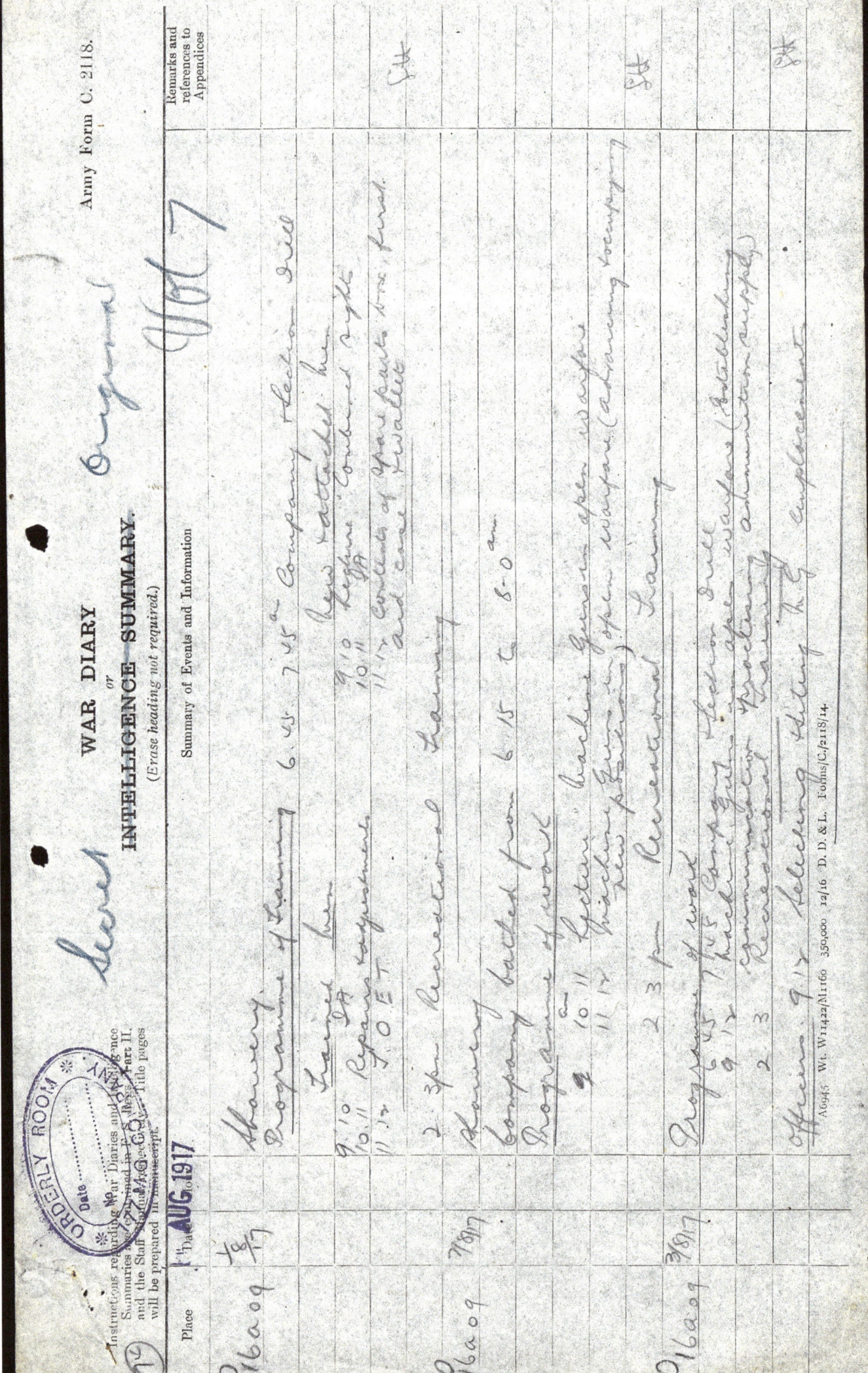

WAR DIARY
INTELLIGENCE SUMMARY

Army Form C. 2118.

Place	Date	Summary of Events and Information	Remarks and references to Appendices
016a09	4/5/17	Company paraded at 8.15am for Brigade Tactical Scheme	
016a09	5/5/17	Church Parade C of E 10.0 am Roman Catholic 9.30 P.C. 9.0	
016a09	6/8/17	Company paraded at 6.0 am for Battalion Tactical Scheme	
096a09	7/8/17	Programme of work. Company Section Drill 9.10 Target hrs 10.11 Lecture (Hostile aircraft) 11.12 Revolver Drill 2 - 3 pm Recreational Training Officer 9.12 new tactical hrs 9.10 " 10.11 " Gun of rifle (action 11.12 " Gun of rifle drills round 2 - 3 " Barrage work (Lecture & Drill)	

WAR DIARY
INTELLIGENCE SUMMARY

Army Form C. 2118.

Place	Date	Hour	Summary of Events and Information	Remarks and references to Appendices
016a09	8/8/17		Programme of work	
		6.45 – 7.15	Company Section Drill	
			Tower he	
		9.15	Revolver practice	
			box rallys he	
		9.00-11	Bayonet Drill	
		10-11		
		11-12	Stripping	
		2-3	Recreational training	
			Officers 9.12 Barrage work (Lectures & Drill)	S/I
016a09	9/8/17		Programme of work	
		6.45 – 7.45	Company Section Drill	
		9.10	Lecture (Barrage work)	
		10-11	Bayonet Drill	
		11-12	Musketry	
		2-3	Recreational training	
				S/I
016a09	10/8/17		Programme of work	
		6.45 to 7.45 a.m	Company Section Drill	
		9-10	Bayonet Drill	
		10-11		
		11-12	Musketry	
			Regimental Training	S/I

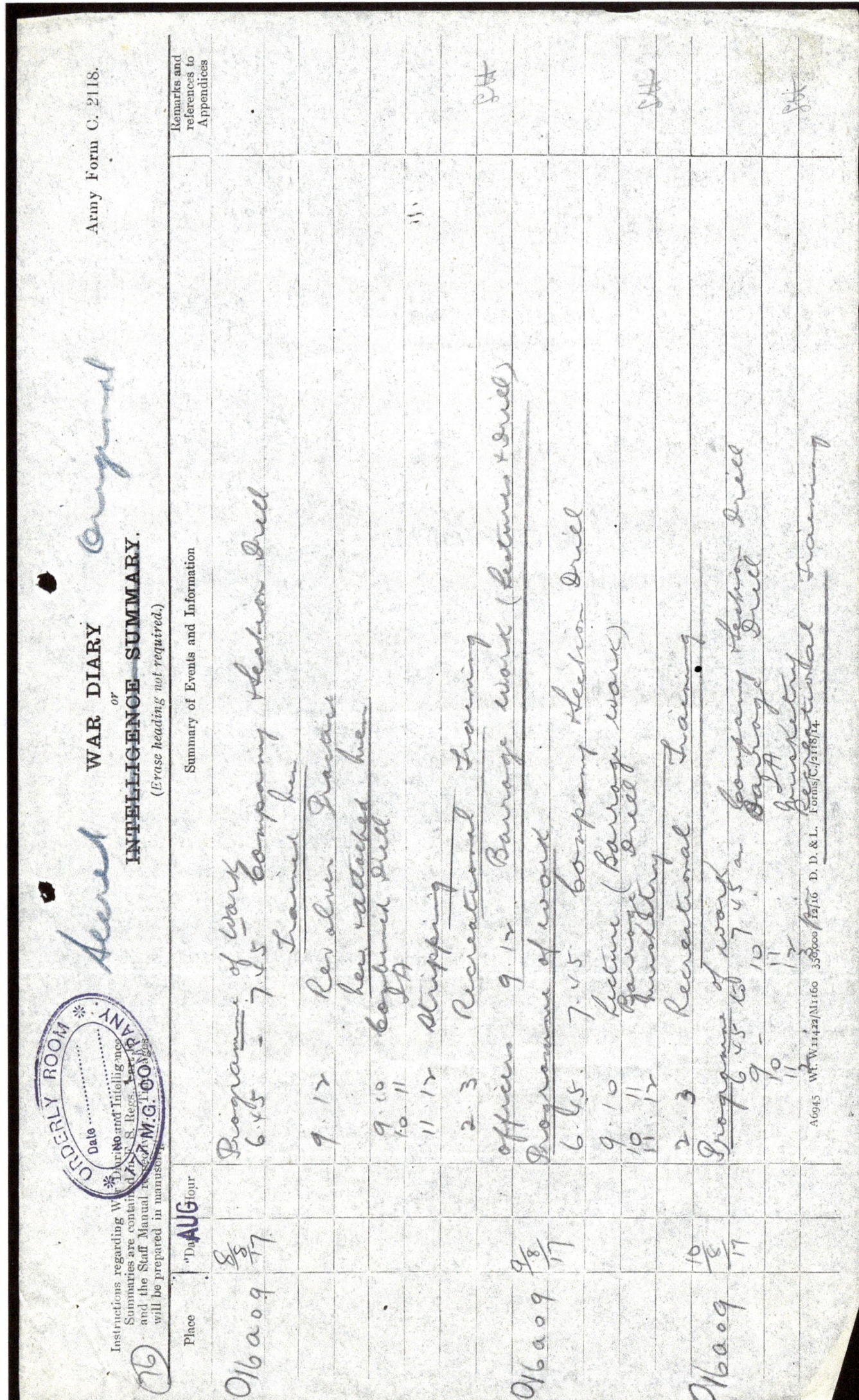

WAR DIARY ~~Secret~~ *original*
or
INTELLIGENCE SUMMARY
(Erase heading not required.)

Army Form C. 2118.

77th M.G. Coy

Place	Date	Summary of Events and Information	Remarks and references to Appendices
O16a09	11/8/17	Company paraded at 5.30 a.m. for Divisional Baraque a ten operation order No. 3 by Capt E.R. King attached	S/L
O16a09	12/8/17	Church Parade CE 10 am Wesleyan 7.30 - RC 9.0 -	S/L
O16a09	13/8/17	Programme of work 6.45 - 7.45 a Company section drill 9.0 " " 10 " " 11 " Lecture. Lewis overhead fire (b) section officers 1 " Continued drill 2.30 h Company bathed	S/L
O16a09	14/8/17	Fine weather - rain in the evening Programme of work 6.15 + 7.45 strip sprockets 10.0 + 7 strip tripods Co. CO, 74 Lincolns + 75 Lincolns No 3 Lewis trained to test attack 10 " Continued drill 11 " Instruction recognition of targets. Above programme was carried out	S/L

Army Form C. 2118.

WAR DIARY
or
INTELLIGENCE SUMMARY.
(Erase heading not required.)

78 Level Original

Instructions regarding War Diaries and Intelligence
Summaries are contained in F.S. Regs., Part II
and the Staff Manual respectively. Title pages
will be prepared in manuscript.

7th M.G. COMPANY

ORDERLY ROOM
Date ....
1 AUG 1917

Place	Date	Hour	Summary of Events and Information	Remarks and references to Appendices
O 16.a.09	15/8/17		Changeable weather. Programme of work.	
		6.45	7 & 5 Company Drill	
			(except for)	
		9.11	Barrage Drill. New attached Gun Officers	
			9 to Lecture. Indirect overhead fire	
		10.11	L.M.	
		11.12	Internal Lecture Gun Officers lectured to officers	∅
			N.C.O.s	
		2.3	Recreational training	
			(hockey) (Special Day).	
			Above programme was carried out	
O 16.a.09	16/8/17		Changeable weather. Programme of work.	
		6.45	7 & 5 Company then Sect	
			Drill + new attached being	
		9.1-	instructed in construction of M.G. Emplacements	
		2.3	Recreational training.	∅
			Company paraded as guard for night operation with	
			Brigade.	
			Above programme was carried out	
O 16.a.09	17/8/17		Changeable weather. Programme of work.	
		7.30 am	Parade 7.30 am for Field Firing. Above programme was carried out	∅

WAR DIARY or INTELLIGENCE SUMMARY

Army Form C. 2118.

227 M.G. COMPANY

Place	Date	Hour	Summary of Events and Information	Remarks and references to Appendices
016a09	13/8/17		Changeable weather. Programme of work:	
		6.45-7.45	Company Section Drill	
			Lewis bus	
		9.10	"	
		10.11	Cartridge of gun	
			Spare parts of gun	
		11.12	Anti gas measures	
			Anti gas measures	
			Above programme was carried out	
016a09	19/8/17		Fine weather - a little rain	
			Church parade	
			Party	
			to	
			9.30	
			a m	
016a09	20/8/17		Fine weather	
			Programme of work	
		9.10	Lecture of elements	
		10.11	"	
		11.12	Lecture above fire	
		2-3	Recreational training	
		6.45-7.45	Company Section Drill	
			Lewis bus	
		9.15	Sweeping range	
		8.45pm	Parade for Brigade Exercise (Night marching)	
			Above prog. Parade carried out	

Kent **WAR DIARY** Original
or
INTELLIGENCE SUMMARY.
(Erase heading not required.)

Army Form C. 2118.

Instructions regarding War Diaries and Intelligence Summaries are contained in F.S. Regs., Part II. and the Staff Manual respectively. Title pages will be prepared in manuscript.

[Stamp: ORDERLY ROOM * 177 M.G. COMPANY]

Place	Date	Summary of Events and Information	Remarks and references to Appendices
O 16.a.09	1 AUG 1917 21/8/17	Fine weather. Programme of work carried out. 9.10 Reveillé 10.11 Gun drill 11.12 Lecture - Hints & Complaints 2pm Cleaning fouling tubes 5-6 By Pulleys 6-7.30 Battery Parade Above programme was carried out	PH
O 16.a.09	22/8/17	Fine day Sections 1 & 3 HQ paraded 3.15am marched to halfway Rest House Section 2 & Lewis 6.45 & left BARASTRE by Motor Bus 7.30am Disembarked at halfway rendezvous Nos 1 & 3 HQ completed journey to Izzelis by Motor Bus No. 2 & L completed journey on foot to rendezvous	PH
Izzelis	23/8/17	Full day Programme of work 9.10 " " 10.11 " " 11.12 Battery Sports Parade Above programme was carried out	PH

A 645. Wt. W14422/M1160. 350,000 12/16. D.D.&L. Forms/C/2118/14.

Army Form C. 2118.

WAR DIARY *seen (original)*
or
INTELLIGENCE SUMMARY.
(Erase heading not required.)

Place	Date	Hour	Summary of Events and Information	Remarks and references to Appendices
Sanlis	24/8/17		Dull day Parade	A
Sanlis	25/8/17		6.40 am for route march All transport fully loaded Dull changeable weather Programme of work 7 - 8 Section Drill 9 - 10 Barrage Drill 10 - 11 Anti gas measures 11 - 12 Use of Plunometer. Each aircraft sight above programme was carried out	A
Sanlis	26/8/17		Fine day Church Parade C 10 am D 9.15 am horses etc 9 am	A
Sanlis	27/8/17		Dull day - changeable Parade 6.15 am for gas by mules 6.45 am for route march full marching order with pack mules	A

77 M.G. Company

Army Form C. 2118.

kept original

WAR DIARY
or
INTELLIGENCE SUMMARY
(Erase heading not required.)

Instructions regarding War Diaries and Intelligence
Summaries are contained in F. S. Regs. Part VII.
and the Staff Manual respectively. Title headings
will be prepared in manuscript.

Army Form No. 67 M.G. Company

Place	Date	Summary of Events and Information	Remarks and references to Appendices
Senlis	28/8/17	Dull – showery day. Programme of work:- 7.8 Section Drill 9.10 Gymnasia 10.11 " 11.12 Packing mules Above programme of work was carried out	
Senlis	29/8/17	Dull showery day Programme of work 8.9 Company Section Drill 9.10 Bayonet fighting 10.11 Wg tactics 11.12 Lecture on Cholera attack above programme was carried out	Stf
Senlis	30/8/17	Dull changeable weather Programme of work 8.9 Company Section Drill 9.10 Bayonet Drill 10.11 Mechanism 11.12 Anti gas measures Company paraded at 8.30 p.m. marched off 8.40 pm to ALBERT & entrained. Left Albert 1.20 am on the 31st	Stf

A.9945. Wt. W.11422/M.1160. 350,000 12/16 D. D. & L. Forms/C/2118/14.

WAR DIARY
or
INTELLIGENCE SUMMARY

Army Form C. 2118.

August

Place	Date	Hour	Summary of Events and Information	Remarks and references to Appendices
Albert	31/8/17		Quiet day. Stand off. Albert 1.a.a. Arrived PROVEN Siding. Trained from PROVEN through WATOU to WINNEZEELE arriving de tulis where Winnezeele 6.30 p.m. Kept north of Battle. J9.a.1.8 — J9.c.5.6 — J9.a.4.3 — J9.c.0.4	
			E.R. King Capt. O.C. No. 177 M.G. Coy.	

Copy No 12

Operation Order No 3
by Capt. G.R King
Commanding 177. Machine Gun Coy.
11-8-17

Map. Ref 57C. S.W

1. The 100th Division of XXX Corps captured on 10-8-17 the enemy's trenches as far as TREACLE TRENCH; the 200th Division on its right has captured the portions of FURIES TRENCH & GALLIA TRENCH in U.2., & the 300th Division on its left has advanced as far as WEST STREET in LE TRANSLOY.

2. The 200th & 100th Divisions will advance at zero hour on the 11-8-17 & capture & consolidate the line PROMETHEUS TRENCH, O.3.2. central, WINDMILL MOUND, the QUARRY (O.31.a.5.9).

The 59th. Division will then pass through the 100th. Division, & with the 200th & 300th. Divisions will capture & consolidate the general line BRUNEHAUT TRENCH (from its junction with the Railway O.34.d.6.6) ROCQUIGNY, BOCHE TRENCH, SUGAR FACTORY.

The 178th Brigade will form the right attack & 177th Brigade the left attack.

3. The objectives of the 59th. Division are:-
   1st Objective   ROCQUIGNY TRENCH – JASON TRENCH – enclosure at O.25.c.7.6
   2nd Objective   The South-east of ROCQUIGNY (as far as the road running N.W. to S.E. through O.27.c.5.8) & BOCHE TRENCH to its junction with the road in T.25.b.0.6

4. 177th Brigade will attack on a 3 battalion frontage:-
   Right   4th Leicesters
   Centre   4th Lincolns
   Left   5th Leicesters
Boundaries as on map marked "A"
Assaulting Battalions will form up for attack in our Front line, support line, & reserve, trenches.
Assaulting troops will advance at Zero in artillery formation till about 200 yds beyond TREACLE TRENCH. Care must be taken that troops for first objective are close up under barrage at zero plus 70.
   Battalion Headquarters as under:-
      4th Leicesters   U.1.a.5.0
      4th Lincolns   T.6.b.8.3
      5th Leicesters   T.6.b.4.7

177 Machine Gun Coy

5. O.C. No 2 Section will detail 2 guns to 7/4 Leicester Regt. & 2 guns to 7/4 Lincoln Regt.

O.C. No 1 Section will detail 2 guns to 7/5 Leicester Regt.

O.C. No 3 Section (including 2 guns of No 1 Section) will select positions in O.31.c on high ground in neighbourhood of

177 Machine Gun Coy (Cont'd)	5	MOON TRENCH from which to bring covering fire on to JASON TRENCH. On capture of JASON TRENCH these guns will move forward to select positions to aid in Consolidating JASON TRENCH. No 4 Section will be in reserve & will move with reserve Battalion
Dress	6	Fighting Order.
Carrying Parties	7	Arrangements will be made for carrying parties & will be detailed to Sections.
Ammunition Supply	8	On reaching their final objective Section Officers will organise further Ammunition dumps & will be responsible that the chain of Ammunition supply is in perfect working order. An officer will be detailed for this task. Positions of new dumps will be forwarded to Company Headquarters. R.E. material & tools will be drawn from Battalion dumps by arrangement with C.O's.
Communication	9	Communication between Company & Section H.Q. will be maintained by visual signalling, also a well organised system of runners & will be arranged beforehand
Positions of Headquarters	10	177 Infantry Brigade Battle Headquarters will open at 8.30 am Aug. 11th at T.6.b.3.7. 177 Machine Gun Coy Headquarters will be at T.6.b.2.2.
Zero Hour	11	Zero Hour will be at 9.0 am Aug 11th. An officer will attend at Water Tanks (C.31.b.u.) at 7.0 am Aug 11th for the synchronisation of watches
	12	Acknowledge

G.R. King Capt
O.C. 177 M.G.Coy

Issued by Special D.R. at
Copy No 1 177 Infty. Bgde H.Q.
       2 O.C. 74 Lincolns
       3 "   75   do
       4 "   74 Leicesters
       5 "   75   do
       6 177 Lt. T.M.B
       7 No 1. Section
       8   " 2   "
       9   " 3   "
      10   " 4   "
      11 Transport Officer
      12 War Diary
      13 War Diary
      14 File

Original 177 M.G. Coy Secret Vol 8

WAR DIARY
or
INTELLIGENCE SUMMARY

Army Form C. 2118.

(Erase heading not required.)

Place	Date	Hour	Summary of Events and Information	Remarks and references to Appendices
Sqr. I. 8 sidi 27 Belgium	1/9/17		Sunday Programme of work:- 6.45 7.45 cleaning billets Lecture Barrage 9 — 10 1A 10 " 1A 11 " 13 Lecture – First aid New totalhi hr 9 " 10 2A 10 " 11 hystemare 11 " 1 Gun Drill above programme of work was carried out	
29.a.1.8	2/9/17		Fine day Church parade C.F. homeoforward 9.45am 9.30	Sit
29.d.1.8	3/9/17		Bright day Programme of work issued ha 9 " 10 1A 10 " 11 Lecture First aid 11 " 12 Gun and Drill 6.45 7.45 Coy section drill Rest of day has per programme 9 " 10 hystemare 10 " 11 Barrage Drill 11 " 12 Two sections were attached to Infantry for tactical scheme above programme was carried out	Sit

177 M.G. COMPANY

WAR DIARY *or* **INTELLIGENCE SUMMARY**
Army Form C. 2118.

Place: Onspach
177 M.G. Coy

Date	Hour	Summary of Events and Information	Remarks and references to Appendices
19.d.1.8.17		Drill day. Programme of work Company drill. Barrage shoot.	
		Revision of—	
	9.10	Barrage Drill	
	10.11	Packing & unpacking limber	
	11.12	Anti gas helmets – Coy Sjt M.G.O	
		Two sections were attached to infantry for tactical exercise	S/H
19.d.1.8.17 5/9/17		Full day. Programme of work 6.45–7.45 Company drill. Revision of—	
	9.10	Barrage Drill	
	10.11	Gun Mounting	
	11.12	Lecture Emplacements	S/H
		Two sections were attached to infantry for tactical exercise. Above programme was carried out.	
19.d.1.8.17 6/9/17		Full day – a little rain. Programme of work Company section drill. Two attached Coy.	
	9.10	Barrage Drill	
	10.11	Lecture (Use of ground cover)	
	11.12	Gas helmets	
		Two sections were attached to infantry for tactical exercise. Above programme was carried out.	S/H

WAR DIARY
INTELLIGENCE SUMMARY

Army Form C. 2118.

Original   Seret

Place	Date	Hour	Summary of Events and Information	Remarks and references to Appendices
19d.1.8.	7/8/17		Dull day – a little rain Programme of work	
			Lewis Gun Drill	
		9.10	Bayonet fight	
		10.11	Drill } 9.10 – 10.11 Company Lewis Gun Drill	
		11.12	Use of Bombing } 10.11 – 11.12 Bayonet fighting	
			11.12 Stripping Vickers gun	
			Two sections were attached to infantry for tactical exercise	S/A
19d.1.8.	8/8/17		Hot sultry day. Programme of work:	
		9.10	Bayonet Fighting } 9.10 – 10.11 Company Lewis Gun Drill	
		10.11	Eclipse h.P.B. open warfare } 10.11 – 11.12 Lecture Characteristics	
		11.12	Control Drill Care & cleaning	
			Two sections were attached to infantry for tactical exercise	S/A
19d.1.8.	9/8/17		Church Parade	
		9.45 am		
		9.45	Concert	S/A
19d.1.8.	10/8/17		Hot sultry day. Backing 6.0 am Gun attached to Limbers	
		9.30–10	Lewis Gun Drill } 9.30–10 Bayonet Drill	
		10.11	Bayonet Drill } 10.11 Mechanism	
		11.12	Practice in use of Poolowdrey } 11.12 Open Parts	
			A few programmes of work was carried out	S/A

WAR DIARY or INTELLIGENCE SUMMARY

Army Form C. 2118.

Original Secret

177 M.G. Company

Place	Date	Hour	Summary of Events and Information	Remarks and references to Appendices
19.d.1.8	1/9/17		Drill day	
		6.45 - 7.45	Company Lecture Drill	
			Inspect Mgs	
		9.10 - 10.11	Pairing & Recog. of targets } New attacked hr	
		10.11 - 11.17	} Gun drill	Ap
		11.17 -	} Contents of spare parts	
		2 - 3 p	Recreational training	
19.d.1.8	12/9/17		Drill day	
		6.45 - 7.45	Company lecture Drill	
			Inspect hr	
		9.10 - 10.11	Gun drill } New attacked hr	
		10.11 - 11.17	Indirect firing at target } Gun drill	Ap
		11.17 -	} Contents of spare parts	
		2 - 3 p	Recreational training	
19.d.1.8	13/9/17		Drill, cleep day	
		1 - 2	Iron hygiene route march, foundry work tactical	
		2 - 3	& bivouac	
		3 p	Rifle Inspection	
			above programme was carried out	Ap

Army Form C. 2118.

Original

WAR DIARY
or
INTELLIGENCE SUMMARY.
(Erase heading not required.)

Place......... Neuve

Date	Hour	Summary of Events and Information	Remarks and references to Appendices
Jan 1 17		Full day Programme of work	
	6.45-7	General Charges	
	7-9	Extra duties	attached two 6th & 7th Company lecture send
	9-10	Range drill	
	10-11	Operators - Telephone	9 & 10 Coys Gun drill
	11-12	Targets	11-12 contents of spare parts bags
	2-3	Lectures Training	
		Above programme was carried out	
Jan 1-8 5/1/17		Above day Company paraded at 5.45 am for Bryant track log	
Jan 1-8 6/1/17		Fine day Gas	
		Church parade	
	9.45 am	CE	
	9.45 am	RC	
Jan 1-8 7/1/17		Fine day Programme of work	
	6.15-7.05	Issued tea - short route march Company	

Wt. W14422/M1160 350,000 12/16 D.D. & L. Forms/C/2118/14.

Army Form C. 2118.

Original Copy

WAR DIARY or INTELLIGENCE SUMMARY.

(Erase heading not required.)

Instructions regarding War Diaries and Intelligence Summaries are contained in F. S. Regs., Part II. and the Staff Manual respectively. Title pages will be prepared in manuscript.

177 M.G. Coy

Place	Date	Hour	Summary of Events and Information	Remarks and references to Appendices
Jq.d.18	6/8/17		Issued here Attacked her 9.10 Barrage Drill 9.10 Gun Drill 10.11 Infantry vocab 10.11 Mechanism 11-12 Camp Guard drill 11-12 " 2-3p Recreational training Above programme of work was carried out	
			Rest day	
Jq.d.18	7/8/17		Programme of work 6.45 - 7.45 Company Kitchen Drill Issued here Attacked her 9.10 Lecture use of ground 9.10 L.g 10.11 " 10.11 Stripping 11.12 Lewis gun 11.12 Lecture & characteristics 2-3p Recreational training above programme of work was carried out	St
			free day Programme of work Issued here Attacked her	
Jq.d.18	8/8/17		6.45 - 7.45 Bail Rouse bayonets wandering gun 9-10 Barrage Drill	St

Army Form C. 2118.

WAR DIARY
or
INTELLIGENCE SUMMARY.

(Erase heading not required.)

Original   Kemmel

Place	Date	Hour	Summary of Events and Information	Remarks and references to Appendices
	19.d.1.8		Fatigue day attached to 10.11 Infantry lectures 11.15 Practical use of panel { 6.45 - 7.15 Carrying apparatus into pits not yet in position { 9 - 10 " { 10 - 11 " { 11 - 12 gun drill	Sh
		2/9/17		
			2.30 Cleaning Laundry/baths above programme was carried out	
	19.d.1.8	2/9/15	Kemmel Rainy day Grade 2 - parade 4.40	
			Company left billets for OUDEZEELE (near to billets L.15.c. 9.1. (Sheet 27 Belgium & France) near POPERINGHE. Arrived at billets 10.45am	Sh
	L.15. 6.9.1.4	3/9/17	Fine day Programme of work 9.10 Cleanliness lecture 10.11 Target hits 11.11 Bayonet drill 11.15 Lewis Gun { 10.11 Lewis Gun { 11.12 heavy gun 2-3 Recreational training. above programme was carried out	Sh

WAR DIARY
INTELLIGENCE SUMMARY

Army Form C. 2118.

		Summary of Events and Information	Remarks and references to Appendices
L15.B.9.1.	1/8/17	Fine day Programme of work	
		6.45- 7.45 Company Section Drill	
		Transferred	
		9.10 Sections attached to ? Division in the use of elevating staff	
		10.11 Lecture to C. in attack (9.10 Division in elevating staff)	
		11.12 Cave clearing 10.11	
		11.12 Cave clearing of guns	
		2.3 Kit inspection by Section Officers	#
		Above programme of work was carried out	
L15.B.9.1.	2/8/17	Fine day	
		Company paraded at 10.45 approached to ? CHADDERSTON Station zero opening at 1.40pm advanced Howitzk 2pm worked to terminus at Goulfid Chateau	#
Goulfid Chateau	3/8/17	Fine day Capt Stithing worked trucks to make arrangement for relief N° 1 & 2 Sections took part in practice attack	#

Army Form C. 2118.

Original

WAR DIARY
or
INTELLIGENCE SUMMARY.

(Erase heading not required.)

Instructions regarding War Diaries and Intelligence
Summaries are contained in F. S. Regs., Part II.
and the Staff Manual respectively. Title pages
will be prepared in manuscript.

Place	Date	Hour	Summary of Events and Information	Remarks and references to Appendices
Goldfish Chateau	24/9/17		with 74 & 75 Lincolns. No 1st Lectures paraded at 7.15 pm to moved to trenches for relief. No 3 Section marched off at 7.30pm to report to O.C. 209th Coy. No 2 Section marched off with 75 Lincoln men for reconnaissance in trenches with battalion — attached find copy of relief orders to 9th Lincoln	A
Trenches	25/9/17		Fine day — Bright light. Relief was completed at 7.30am. Operation order No 7 issued to section — copy attached	A
Trenches	26/9/17		Fine day — visibility good. Company took part in offensive operations, see attached appendix for details.	A
Trenches	27/9/17		Weather fine. See attached appendix for details.	A

Army Form C. 2118.

WAR DIARY
or
INTELLIGENCE SUMMARY.

(Erase heading not required.)

Original   Level

Place: M.G. COMPANY

Date	Hour	Summary of Events and Information	Remarks and references to Appendices
Trenches 28/9/17		Fine weather. See attached appendix for details	—
Trenches 29/9/17		Fine weather. See attached appendix for details	—
Trenches 30/9/17		Fine weather. See appendix for details. Company was relieved by 2nd New Zealand M.G. Coy. Relief completed at 11.43 p.m.	—

E.A. King Capt.
O.C. No. 177 M.G. Coy.

Appendix to War Diary for
month of September 1917
for 177 Machine Gun Coy

Report on operations from 24th
to 30 Sept. 1917
Map Ref Sheet 28. N.W.

On the night of 24/25 Sept, 8 guns of 177 Machine Gun Coy relieved the guns of 2 sections of 174 Machine Gun Company.

No 2 Section was accommodated in trenches occupied by 2/4 + 2/5 Lincolns.

No 3 Section was ordered to report to O.C. 200 M.G.Coy for Barrage work. Rations for 48 hours plus emergency ration were carried by the men.

Guides were detailed by 174 M.G.Coy to meet 1 + 4 Sections at C.28.b.2.5. + guide them to Section HQ.

The relief was completed by 7.5 a.m.

During the day of 25th operation orders for 26th were received + issued to Sections.

No 1 Section was ordered to report to O.C. 2/4 Lincolns.

No 2 Section was ordered to report to O.C. 2/5 Lincoln

No 4 Section was ordered to report to 2/4 2/5 Leicesters detailing 2 guns to each Battalion.

These sections were placed under the control of O.C. Battalions.

During the night 25/26 September sections took up positions of assembly behind their respective Battalions before 4 a.m.

After the attack commenced No 4 Section moved forward to consolidate with infantry at Zero hour

No 1 Section moved forward at ZERO plus 95 mins

No 2 Section moved forward at ZERO plus 100 minutes

During the advance No 4 Section reached their 1st objective with 3 guns in action. The remaining gun was put out of action.

One gun was at point D20.b.5.0, one gun at point D20.b.5.1 & the 3rd gun at D14.d.4.2.

No 1 Section moved up into position when infantry had taken final objective & selected positions in front of DOCHY FARM at D20.b.80.95. D20.b.90.85 and D21.c.10.85.

During the advance one gun was put out of action. The Section Officer being wounded, section sergeant immediately assumed command.

No 2 Section moved up into position after the infantry had taken final objective & aided in consolidation.

Two guns were placed in No 2 Strong point at D14.d.65.55.

Remaining two guns were under the command of an N.C.O who had been directed where to place his guns. This N.C.O was killed, & one gun was put out of action during the advance. Other casualties were suffered & a composite team was formed out of the remainder, which dug in at point D20.b.35.45.

This gun eventually came under the command of O.C. No 4 Section.

During the evening of the 26th. the enemy counter-attacked but was driven off by artillery & machine gun barrage.

One gun at No 2 Strong Point was put out of action but O.C. No 2 Section came across a gun of 175 M.G.Coy near Strong Point No 2 & placed it under his command. This was notified to O.C. company concerned.

The morning of the 27th between the hours of about 5 & 7 am the enemy put down a heavy barrage during which one gun of No 1 Section was put out of action leaving 2 guns in action to this section.

About 8.30 am communication was established between No 1 & 4 Sections & Company HQ.

It was not until the evening of the

27th that communication was established between No 2 Section & company H.Q.

The difficulties experienced being on a/c of the heavy enemy barrage & casualties inflicted on runners

On the evening of the 27th enemy again counter-attacked. This attack was dispersed by our artillery barrage

The two machine guns at No 1 Strong point engaged the enemy (estimated at about 200 strong) at a range of 1100 yards & inflicted casualties.

On the night of 27th orders were received from Division to send one officer & two complete gun teams from the transport lines to relieve two guns of 215 M.G.Coy at Cluster Cottages.

Relief was completed by 2 am

On the morning of the 28th the enemy again shelled our positions between the hours of 6 & 8 am

Nothing of importance occurred during the day

Continuously during the night 28/29th enemy shelled our positions with H.E. & gas shells. Seven men of our ration party were gassed

As the frontage was extended during the night 27/28th, No 3 Section was ordered to move forward with 2 guns on evening of 28th.

One gun to occupy No 3 Strong point at D.14.d.10.85 & the other gun at MARTHA HOUSE at D.14.c.35.60

These positions were occupied by 10.5 p.m.

Also on the same night one gun of No 4 Section from D.20.b.5.1. was ordered to move to No 3 Strong point at D.14.d.10.85. This movement was carried out by 10.53 p.m

On the night of 29/30 the two guns at Cluster Cottages were relieved by two gun teams of the 2nd New Zealand M.G.Coy.

On the night of 30/1st Oct the company was relieved by the 2nd New Zealand M.G.Coy.

177 Machine Gun Coy.

Addendum to appendix to War Diary for September 1917

Re operations from 24/30 Sept.

Insert on page "5" after "line 28"

On 28th, Information being received that DOCTY FARM was in our possession, the two guns remaining of No 1 Section pushed forward at dusk & occupied positions at D.21.a.25.85 and D.15.c.05.15.

On the morning of the 29th, information was received from Gun at D.21.a.15.85 that a hostile machine gun was located at ISRAEL HOUSE in D.21.a.65.70, also indications showed that ISRAEL HOUSE was being used as a Headquarters by some unit. This information was forwarded to the artillery through Brigade Headquarters. The following morning ISRAEL HOUSE was subjected to a fierce bombardment.

E.R. King
O.C. No. 177 M.G. Coy.

The relief was completed by 11.43 pm, & company arrived at Transport lines G.5.C.6.4. at 2.15 am 17th Oct.

Ammunition

Ammunition was obtained by the Company from dumps formed at ELMS Corner & SPREE Farm & from S.A.A. boxes obtained from infantry, also from bandoliers found on dead & wounded men.

Rations

Rations & water were brought up to POMMERN Castle (Company H.Q.) & were distributed to sections from this point.

Casualties

The Total casualties during these operations, incurred by the unit were:—

	Officers	O. Ranks
Killed	—	8
Wounded	1	19
Missing	—	3
Gassed	—	9
Shell shock	—	1

Machine Guns in the recent Operations

I Use made of Machine Guns.
(a) Used to aid in consolidation of objectives gained.
(b) Protecting flanks against counter attacks.
(c) Direct overhead fire
(d) Guns in front line were often used to engage targets at 1000 yds range & over with good effect. Observation of fire was easily obtained & guns ranged accordingly
(e) Hostile troops were seen to collect

preparatory to counter attack &
were dispersed by skilful use of our
machine guns.

II Lessons learned.

The following points which were
practised in training were emphasized
(a) Communication between company HQ &
sections most important (Good &
adequate supply of runners essential)
(b) Communication between gun teams &
Section HQ also important.
Men should be impressed with the
necessity for communicating their
position to Section officer in the event
of the latter being unable to locate
them, especially under the conditions
which existed in the recent operations.
(c) Use of ground & cover was greatly
emphasized during the operations.
(d) The formation of gun teams.
During the advance it is suggested
that artillery formation should be
maintained, as, under present conditions
it facilitates communication & control.
One gun team which adopted extended
order arrived minus gun & tripod.
(e) Range-finders
It has been suggested by Section Officers
who were in the front line that range-
finders would have been extremely useful.
This was partially overcome by
observation made practicable by
configuration & state of the ground.
One section did take a range-finder &
found it extremely useful.

E. R. King, Capt. OC
17th M.G. Coy

WAR DIARY
or
INTELLIGENCE SUMMARY

Army Form C. 2118.

(Erase heading not required.)

1797 M.G. Coy

Place	Date	Summary of Events and Information	Remarks and references to Appendices
G5.c.6.c. Hyde 28SW Bay	1/10/17	Fine sunny day. Horses watered at Transport lines before 2am. Reveille 12 noon. 2pm Roll call & packing limbers	
G5.c.6.c	2/10/17	Fine bright day. Transport Section left for en route to Berguin 8.15 & arrived at G5 C.6 & en route to Berguin by march route. 9 Section left for St Venant. Remainder of Company of 2 officers 81 O.R. reported to R.T.O. Haverskerque station at 12 midday & marched to station. Remainder of Company paraded at 12 midday marched to station. Company entrained at 3.30pm, detrained at THIENNES 5.15am 3/10/17	
St Venant	3/10/17	Dull & very day. Detrained 1.30 am Company arrived at Billets near St Venant at 5.15 am. Reveille 12 noon. No parades	
St Venant	4/10/17	Dull showery day. Parades. 17 Section engaged returns of deficiencies due to company officers. Indigestion detected to company officers submitted. 2.3p recreational training	

WAR DIARY or INTELLIGENCE SUMMARY

Army Form C. 2118.

Place	Date	Hour	Summary of Events and Information	Remarks and references to Appendices
ST. VENANT	5/10/17		Fine day. Fresh breezy. Trainprogramme of work:—	
		9-9.45 am	P.T. Peletoon	
		10-11	Sqdn Drill	
		11-12	Sqdn P.T.A	
		3	Ceremonial turnout	
			The above programme was carried out.	
ST. VENANT	6/10/17		Rainy day. No 1 & 2 Sqdns paraded 5.45 am & proceeded by road route to COTTES via ST HILAIRE. No 3rd Sqdron proceeded at 7.30 am & marched to two points nearer on LILLERS - ST VENANT Rd. where they entrained - detrained at COTTES made by two St Hilaire. No 1 & 2 Sqdns rode by two & Billets in ERNY ST JULIEN. No 3rd Sqdn bivouaced to ERNY ST JULIEN by road route. arrived about 3pm Transport paraded at 7.30 a proceeded under Transport officer & arrangements by road route to ERNY ST JULIEN arriving 3 p.m.	※
ERNY ST JULIEN	7/10/17		Rainy day. Paraded Church parade - Cty. 10.15 am Holy Communion in officers mess after service. Watches time adopted 1 am 8/10/17	※

Army Form C. 2118.

WAR DIARY
or
INTELLIGENCE SUMMARY.
(Erase heading not required.)

Place	Date	Hour	Summary of Events and Information	Remarks and references to Appendices
Coy H Julien	6/10/17		Changeable weather. Employed of coy at	
		9-12.30	Cleaning guns Lewis checking spare parts	YB
		2.30-3.30 pm	reorganation of gun teams. Recreational training	
Coy H Julien	7/10/17		Changeable weather. Occasional bright periods followed by heavy showers. Employ of coys —	
		6.45		
		7.45	Company station drill	YB
		10	medical	
		11	"	
		4	Barrage drill	
Coy H Julien	10/10/17	1.30		
		3.30	Packing limbers in preparation for move	YB
			Rainy weather. Company paraded marched off at 7am proceeding to BOURS arriving 3.30 p.m. and there to BOURS	
BOURS	11/10/17		Changeable weather. Company paraded marched off at 4pm proceeding by march route to MAISNEL-LES-RUITZ arriving 5.30pm	YB

WAR DIARY or **INTELLIGENCE SUMMARY**
Army Form C. 2118.

Place	Date	Hour	Summary of Events and Information	Remarks and references to Appendices
MAISNEL LES RUITZ	12/10/17		Changeable weather. Confirmation marched off at 9.30am proceeded by route route to camp at CARENCY	
Carency	13/10/17		Changeable weather. Parades	
	14/10/17		7.10 Inspection of Box respirators gas appliances ammunition &c 10.11 Company Parade 11.12.30 Arm Drill & Physical 2–4 Cleaning Billets	
Carency	14/10/17		Changeable weather. Company paraded at 5pm marched off at 5.30pm for trenches. Relieved 13th Coy in E Coy in AVION Sector. Relief complete 2am 15/10/17 Targets engaged during the night 2000 rds expended	
Trenches	15/10/17		Changeable weather. Targets were engaged during the night 6,750 rds fired	
Trenches	16/10/17		Fine weather. Fresh wind. Targets were engaged during the night number of rounds fired 11,750	

WAR DIARY
or
INTELLIGENCE SUMMARY.

Army Form C. 2118.

Place	Date	Hour	Summary of Events and Information	Remarks and references to Appendices
Trenches	17/10/17		Fine weather. Targets were engaged during the night, number of rounds expended 6,250.	A8
Trenches	18/10/17		Fine weather, french wind. Targets were engaged during the night number of rounds expended 10,750.	A8
Trenches	19/10/17		Fine weather. Targets were engaged during the night. Number of rounds expended 10,080.	A8
Trenches	20/10/17		Fine weather. Targets were engaged during the night. Number of rounds fired 16,500.	A8
Trenches	21/10/17		Fine weather. Harassing fire was used during the night, number of rounds fired 8,000.	A8
Trenches	22/10/17		Fine weather. Company guns relieved in the Avion Sector by 175 Machine Gun Coy. Relief completed at 11.30 p.m. Company marched back to camp by sections.	A8

WAR DIARY
or
INTELLIGENCE SUMMARY.

Army Form C. 2118.

(Erase heading not required.)

Original

Place	Date	Hour	Summary of Events and Information	Remarks and references to Appendices
Caveney	23/10/17		Fresh wind. showery weather. Equipment arrived from line 2.30 am Retail 10 am Parade 1 pm for inspection 1.15 pm for bathing	
Caveney	24/10/17		Fresh wind showery weather Programme of work	
		6.30		
		10 am	Company to shew park +	
		11	Battery Drill	
		12.30	Coney found drill	
			Above programme was carried out	
Caveney	25/10/17		Changeable weather - fresh wind Programme of work	
		6.30	P.T.	
		10	Cleaning of horses + equipment	
		10.15	Inspection of equipment, iron rations, identity discs	
		to		
		11.		
		11.45	P.T.	
		12.30		
		11.45	P.T.	
			Above programme was carried out	
Caveney	26/10/17		Rainy weather. Programme of work	
		6.30		
		9.30	P.T.	
		12.30	Officers hour occurred in [?], D.A. stripping + cleaning + cleaned	

Army Form C. 2118.

WAR DIARY
or
INTELLIGENCE SUMMARY.
(Erase heading not required.)

Original

Place	Date	Hour	Summary of Events and Information	Remarks and references to Appendices
Caveney	1/10/17		Cold	
		9.30	Reveille	
		10.30	S.D.	
		11.30	Gas Drill	
		12.30	Mechanism	
			Above programme was carried out	S.D.
Caveney	2/10/17		Rainy weather	
			Programme of work	
		9-11	Fitting new containers to box respirators	
		11-11.45	S.D.	
		11.45-12.30	P.T.	S.D.
			Above programme was carried out	
Caveney	17/10/17		Rainy weather	
			Horse of mounted service in camp 9.30 am	S.D.
Caveney	23/10/17		Rainy weather	
		6.30	P.T.	
		9.30		
		7.30	No. 1 Company repairing huts	
		11.45		
		11.45-12.30	Mechanism	
			Above programme was carried out	S.D.

WAR DIARY
or
INTELLIGENCE SUMMARY.

Army Form C. 2118.

Place	Date	Hour	Summary of Events and Information	Remarks and references to Appendices
Cuency	30/9/17		Changeable weather. Programme of work thus run:-	
		8.30 9.30 a.m	P.T.	
		9.30 10.30	Range cards	
		10.30 11.30	Sighting drill	
		11.30 12.30	Course of No.1 stoppage	
		2.30 3.30 p.m	Overhead fire	
Cuency	1/10/17		A fine but cold day. Programme of work thus:-	
		8.30 9.30	P.T.	
		9.30 10.30	Agent parts	
		10.30 11.30	Clinometer drill Elevation	
	2/10/17		Travel me	
		8.30 9.30	P.T.	
		9.30 10.30	do	
		10.30 11.30	Lecture	
		11.30 12.30	Barrage drill	
	3/10/17		Travel me	
		8.30 9.30	P.T.	
		9.30 10.30	Sighting drill	
		10.30 11.30	Lecture: Overhead fire	
		11.30 12.30	Practise machine use of Clinometer	

E.A. King Capt.
O.C. No. 177 M.G. Coy.

SECRET
Copy No 8

177th MACHINE GUN COMPANY

OPERATION ORDER No 8

Reference Sheet 1. VIMY 1/10,000
            2. LENS 1/10,000

1. In accordance with 177 Infantry Brigade Operation Order No 58, dated 20th Oct 1917 the 175 Machine Gun Coy will relieve this unit in the AVION SECTOR on the night of Oct 22/23rd in positions as follows:-

SECTION	GROUP + GUN No	MAP LOCATION	RELIEVED BY
4	AMBLE	1. T 2 d 45.60 2. T 2 d 55.60 3. T 3 a 20.25	No 3. SECTION (less 1 gun) 175 M.G.Co
	SECTION. H.Q.S.	T 2 b 20.85	
1	BEAVER	1. T 2 b 58.50 2. T 2 b 22.70 3. T 2 a 80.05 4. T 2 a 40.25	No 4. SECTION 175 M.G.Co
	SECTION. H.Q.S.	T 2 b 20.85	
3	AGENT	1. N 31. d 43.22 2. N 31. d 50.10 3. T 1. c 30.50 4. S 6. b 55.15	No 2 SECTION 175 M.G.Co
	SECTION. H.Q.S.	T 1. d 30.90	
2	ONTARIO	1. N 25 c 75.10 2. N 31 a 85.90 3. N 31 a 35.85 4. M 26 d 37.80	No 1 SECTION 175 M.G.Co
	SECTION. H.Q.S.	M 26 b 50.20	
HIRONDELLE	TACTICAL GUN.	M 26 a 05.40	1 GUN. No 3. SEC 175 M.G.Coy
COMPANY	H.Q.S.	T 1. d. 30.90	

2. Guides

Limber for left sector + HIRONDELLE gun will proceed under arrangements made by 175 M.G. Coy to left sectors dump. Guides left sector (N°2) 177 M.G. Coy will act according to arrangements made between section officers.

Guide from HIRONDELLE tactical gun will wait on KINGSTON RD. at point M35.b.9.5. to detach its relief from limber of left section, 175 M.G. Coy.

Two guides from N°3 Section will meet 175 M.G. Coys limber at junction of VICTORIA RD + LENS-ARRAS RD at 6 p.m. One will take half-limber to point where CYRIL TRENCH passes under LENS ARRAS RD. The other guide will take remaining limber to Company dump.

OC N°3 Section will arrange for one guide per team to meet these limbers at 6.30 p.m.

OC N°1 Section will detail five guides to be at Company dump at 6.30 p.m. to conduct Section HQ + gun teams to their respective positions.

OC N°4 Section will detail one guide to take limber of its relieving section (N°3 Section 175 Coy) to section dump where he will arrange to have one guide per team to conduct relieving teams to their respective positions.

3. Belt boxes & Tripods

Ten belt boxes per gun + the tripod will be handed over to incoming teams, + receipts taken for same. Similar amount will be turned over by the 175 M.G. Coy after relief.

4. Trench Stores

All trench stores, maps +c will be handed over to the relieving unit & receipts taken for same. All petrol tins will be handed over.

5. Situation

Section officers will give relieving officers full particulars regarding situation, fields of fire, S.O.S. lines, lines of fire, night firing targets, + work in progress +c.

6. Completion of relief

Will be reported to Company HQ by runner, who will guide a runner of 175 M.G. Coy to Company HQ.

Transport.   The transport officer will arrange to supply limbers as follows:—

  Two half limbers for No. 3 Section
  One complete limber each for Nos 1, 2, & 4 Sections & Coy HQ.

  These limbers will leave CARENCY one hour after departure of the 175 M.G.Coy on night of 22/23rd Oct.

  Five officers chargers will be at S.12.d.45.05 (old Coy HQ) at 8.30 pm.

  Two officers chargers will be at the gap in railway embankment on the way to No. 2 Section's dump at 8.30 pm.

8   Upon completion of relief, sections will proceed to camp at CARENCY after loading limbers.

  In the event of our limbers arriving late at the dumps, section officers will detail one N.C.O. & two men per section to remain behind to load limbers.

                    W. J. Hawkes 2/Lt
                    for O.C.
                    177 M.G. Coy.

9   Acknowledge.
  Issued by special D.R. at.
  ✓ Copy No 1 O.C. Coy.
       2 OC No 1 & 4 Sections
       3 OC No 2 Section
       4 178 Infty Bde.
       5 Transport Officer
       6 D.M.G.O.
       7 175 M.G. Coy.
       8 War diary.

Operation order by
Capt. G.R.L. ~~~~
Commanding 177th Machine Gun Coy
[ORDERLY ROOM stamp — 177 M.G. COMPANY]
map ref 57cNE 1/40000
sheet Bourlon

On the night of 29/30 Nov 1917
the 177 Machine Gun Coy will
relieve the 7th Motor Machine
Gun Battery & two guns of 174
Machine Gun Coy

No 1 Section will take over 4 guns
of the 7th Motor Machine Gun
Battery
  Two guns of No 4 Section will
take over 2 guns of 174 M Gy Coy

  The remaining two guns of No 4
Section will move into newly
selected positions

  No 2 & 3 Sections will move
into selected positions in
F2d & L2b
  These two sections will
form a battery of 8 guns

  No 1 Section & two guns of

No 4. Section will take over all trench stores, maps, night firing sticks, range cards &c and will give receipts for same.

Completion of relief will be forwarded by runner by code word "PIPE".

Acknowledge.

E.H. King   Capt OC
177 M.G. Coy.

Distribution as follows:-
Copy No 1   OC No 1 Section
     2   " 2   "
     3   " 3   "
     4   " 4   "
     5   War diary
     6   ——
     7   File

WAR DIARY
or
INTELLIGENCE SUMMARY

Army Form C. 2118

ORIGINAL
Confidential
177 M.G. Coy
Nov 1917 Vol 10

Place	Date	Hour	Summary of Events and Information	Remarks and references to Appendices
Caveney	1/11/17		Showery weather. Usual Regimental training:—	
		7.30	Section Drill	
		9.30	Gun Drill	
		10.30	Range Drill	
		11.30	Lecture — chief of Sections on Gun	
				OK
		11.30	Rifle B.S.A	
		12.30		
		2.30		
		3.30		
		4.30	QT	
			A fatigue party of 2 officers + 50 men was employed at Bullecourt from 9am to 5pm.	OK
			Above programme was carried out.	
2/11/17			Fine variable weather.	OK
			Programme of work—	
		8.30		
		9.30	Section Drill	
		10.30	Gun Drill	
		11.30	Indirect fire	OK
		12.30		
		2.30	Strip & clean (musketry instruction, musketry training)	
		3.30		
		4.30	QT	OK
			Officers lecture 2.30-3.30. Interest overhead fire.	
			Fatigue party of one officer + 50 men for Brigade harrow	
			five reinforcements arrived, Lewis.	OK

Army Form C. 2118.

WAR DIARY
or
INTELLIGENCE SUMMARY.
(Erase heading not required.)

Instructions regarding War Diaries and Intelligence Summaries are contained in F.S. Regs., Part II. and the Staff Manual respectively. Title pages will be prepared in manuscript.

Place	Date	Hour	Summary of Events and Information	Remarks and references to Appendices
Quevy	3/11/17		Changeable weather	
			Programme of work	
		8.30		
		9.30	Gas lecture Drill	
		10.30	Musketry (have fired all round harness)	
		11.30	Swedish drill	
		12.30	House of cards	
		1.30	Standing orders	
		3.30	P.T.	
			Afternoon — officers lecture	
			Fatigue parties of one officer & one N.C.O & 30 men for Brigade transport lines from 9 a.m — 8 p.m	
Quevy	4/11/17		Fine day — cold	
			Church parade	
			Fatigue party of 30 men to officers for Brigade fatigue.	
			Capt Guy S.R. visited 2nd in Coy to prior to taking over from him.	
Quevy	5/11/17		Fine cold day	
			Fatigue party joined for Brigade transport lines fatigue of 1 Officer & 30 men (9 & 4 & 5)	
			Programme of work	
		8.30		
		9.30		
		10.30	Company & Section drill	
		11.30	Standing orders	
			6 Lewis gun detachments gone part of all company except that just had draughts for bombs 30 & have been over into the to intermediate firing to take	
			14 number over into line for instruction prior to taking	

Army Form C. 2118.

WAR DIARY
or
INTELLIGENCE SUMMARY.
(Erase heading not required.)

Army Form C. 2118

Instructions regarding War Diaries and Intelligence Summaries are contained in F. S. Regs., Part II. and the Staff Manual respectively. Title pages will be prepared in manuscript.

104 / 177 M.G. COMPANY

Place	Date	Hour	Summary of Events and Information	Remarks and references to Appendices
Caveney	5/11/17		Over from 200 M.Gun on the 6th November	
Aveney	6/11/17		Changeable weather. 8.30. 17 sections preparing prior to going into trenches packing limbers.	
			Returned 4.30 p.m. 200 b/f Coy in trenches. Relay complete by 10.15 p.m. Gunfire was engaged during the night. Rattles of rounds fired 10,000.	OC
Lewis	7/11/17		Changeable weather. The O.C. visited centre group of guns the morning 6 am. 177 M.Go. visited company headquarters also OC 200 b/Coy. 8 gun fired some 12,000 rounds last night. O.C. visited left gun positions 5.25 am	OC
Lewis	8/11/17		Changeable weather. 177 M.Go. visited our HQ. Capt. King & 177 M.Go. visited trenches looking for new positions. 7 gun fired some 11,000 rounds at different targets. OC visited night relief of guns.	OC
Lewis	9/11/17		Cloudy weather. 177 M.Go visited our Company HQ. Capt. King visited trenches with 177 M.Go. 9 gun fired 27,000 rounds during the hours of 7pm & 1am. Suitable targets were engaged. OC visited left sector.	OC

WAR DIARY
or
INTELLIGENCE SUMMARY.
(Erase heading not required.)

Army Form C. 2118.

Place	Date	Summary of Events and Information	Remarks and references to Appendices
LIEVIN	9/11/17	Rainy weather. Harassing fire on enemy tracks during expected raid on Gunderson trenches, round fired 10,000! Harassing fire also brought to bear on the town of Sparie. Rounds fired 7,13,080.	
LIEVIN	10/11/17	Changeable weather. Targets were engaged during the night. 8 guns firing 15,080 rounds.	BJ
LIEVIN	11/11/17	Fine weather. Targets were engaged during the night. 15,000 rounds were fired during the hours of 8pm & 7am.	BJ
LIEVIN	12/11/17	Fine weather. Targets were engaged during the night. Where fired during the hours of 8 — 7am. 15,000 rounds were fired.	BJ
LIEVIN	13/11/17	Fine weather. Targets were engaged during the night firing some 15,000 rounds during the hours of 8 and 6 am.	BJ
LIEVIN	14/11/17	Fine weather. The section in command vicinity own changed to re-making cross roads for night firing on the night of 16/17. Target was engaged during the hours of 7/15pm 6am — 15,000 rounds was fired.	BJ
LIEVIN	15/11/17	Fine weather. OC & MyStaff visited centre group of guns & everything was in good order.	BJ

WAR DIARY
or
INTELLIGENCE SUMMARY.
(Erase heading not required.)

Army Form C. 2118.

Instructions regarding War Diaries and Intelligence Summaries are contained in F. S. Regs. Part II. and the Staff Manual respectively. Title pages will be prepared in manuscript.

Place	Date	Summary of Events and Information	Remarks and references to Appendices
LIEVIN	16/11/17	Relieved by the 13 Canadiers before daylight & company marched back to Ethrupont and & via the 8 WAR ENG:	
GRENAY	17/11/17	Company resting at Carency	
Carency	18/11/17	Marched from Carency to Wanquetin	
Carency	19/11/17	Left Wanquetin about 5 pm marched to Bellacourt	
Bellacourt	20/11/17	Still at Bellacourt the company on ordinary training	
Bellacourt	21/11/17	Left Bellacourt about midnight	
Bellacourt	22/11/17	Arrived at ACHIET le PETIT about 6am the company being on the Prisoners escort & the Guard	
Achiet le Petit	23/11/17	Left camp at 7am & marched to "Achiet le grand" & entrained for Trins Ginine at FINS about 2 pm, marched to Dessart wood where the company went camped.	
Dessart Wood	24/11/17	Still at Dessart Wood, weather very disagreeable.	
Dessart Wood	25/11/17	Still at Dessart Wood, company doing ordinary machine gun training	

Army Form C. 2118.

WAR DIARY
or
INTELLIGENCE SUMMARY.
(Erase heading not required.)

Place	Date	Hour	Summary of Events and Information	Remarks and references to Appendices
Leeward Wood	26/11/17		Still at Leeward Wood	
Leeward Wood	27/11/17		Left Leeward Wood at 1.15 pm marched to REJEGNIT of Company completed Reserve	
Reserve	28/11/17		Left Reserve 2.30 pm marched to FLESQUIERES	
Flesquieres	29/11/17		16 guns went into the line during the afternoon, no important event	
Flesquieres	30/11/17		Our guns were heavily shelled + destroyed	

G.R. King Capt OC
177 M.G. Coy

To O.C. "A" Coy
        Capt. G. R. KING
                177th Machine Gun Coy.

Map
Sheet LENS 36. S.W.1   5-11-1917.
Scale
10,000

1. In accordance with 177th Infantry Brigade Operation Order No 61. dated 4/11/17, the 177th Machine Gun Company will relieve the 200th Machine Gun Company in the LENS Sector on the night of 6/7 Nov./17.

2. The relief will not take place before dark.

GUIDES 3. Guides will meet the Company at 200 Machine Gun Company HQ & will guide the Sections to their respective Section HQ. At Section H.Q. gun teams will be guided to their positions.

DISPOSITION OF SECTIONS 4. No. 2 Section & 2 guns of No 4 Section will occupy the RIGHT GROUP of guns.
No 3 Section will occupy the CENTRE GROUP of guns.
No 1 Section will occupy the LEFT GROUP of guns.
The remaining 2 guns of No 4 Section will be held in reserve at Company H.Q.

SITUATION 5. Section officers will receive full particulars regarding situation, fields of fire, S.O.S. targets, night firing targets &c.

TRENCH STORES 6. All Trench Stores, maps, Petrol Tins &c will be taken over from the Company to be relieved & receipts given for same.

BELT BOXES & TRIPODS 7. All Tripods & 10 belt boxes per gun will be taken over with the exception of the MAXIM GUN which will take over 14 belt boxes. A similar number of belt boxes will be handed over to the 200th Machine Gun Company at transport lines CARENCY.

COMPLETION OF RELIEF 8. Completion of relief will be reported to Company HQ by runner by the code word "PANTS".

9. Acknowledge.

                                        G.R.King Capt. O.C.
                                        177th Machine Gun Coy.

Distribution
Copy No 1   HQ 177 Inf Bgde
      2   OC 200 M.G. Coy
      3   D.M.G.O
      4   OC No 1 Section
      5   "   2   "
      6   "   3   "
      7   "   4   "
      8   Transport Officer
      9   War Diary
     10   do. do.
     11   File

Operation Orders by
Capt. G. KING
Commanding 177th Machine Gun Coy.

Map Ref.
Sheet: LENS 36.S.W.1   5-11-1917.
1/10,000

1. In accordance with 177th Infantry Brigade Operation Order No. 61. dated 4/11/17, the 177th Machine Gun Company will relieve the 200th Machine Gun Company in the LENS Sector on the night of 6/7 Nov.

2. The relief will not take place before dark.

GUIDES 3. Guides will meet the Company at 200 Machine Gun Company HQ & will guide the Sections to their respective Section HQ. At Section HQ. gun teams will be guided to their positions.

DISPOSITION 4. No. 2 Section & 2 guns of No. 4 Section will
OF SECTIONS   occupy the RIGHT GROUP of guns.
              No. 3 Section will occupy the CENTRE GROUP of guns.
              No. 1 Section will occupy the LEFT GROUP of guns.
              The remaining 2 guns of No. 4 Section will be held in reserve at Company HQ.

SITUATION 5. Section officers will receive full particulars regarding situation, fields of fire, S.O.S. targets, night firing targets &c.

TRENCH 6. All Trench Stores, maps, Petrol Tins &c
STORES   will be taken over from the Company to be relieved & receipts given for same.

BELT BOXES 7. All Tripods & 10 belt boxes per gun will
& TRIPODS   be taken over with the exception of the MOULIN GUN which will take over 14 belt boxes. A similar number of belt boxes will be handed over to the 200th Machine Gun Company at Transport Lines CARENCY.

COMPLETION 8. Completion of relief will be reported to
OF RELIEF   Company HQ by runner by the code word "PANTS"

9. Acknowledge.

G.B. King Capt. O.C.
177th Machine Gun Coy.

Distribution
Copy No. 1   HQ 177 Inf Bde
        2   OC 200 MG Coy
        3   D.M.G.O
        4   OC No 1 Section
        5   "   2   "
        6   "   3   "
        7   "   4   "
        8   Transport Officer
        9   War Diary
        10   do.   do.
        11   File

217 M.G.C. Coy original 31st Sept 57C /

Army Form C. 2118.

WAR DIARY
or
INTELLIGENCE SUMMARY.
(Erase heading not required.)

Place	Date	Summary of Events and Information	Remarks and references to Appendices
Hargincourt	DEC 1917 1/17	Our forward Lewis gun were heavily shelled at intervals during the day also Lewis gun and concealed Rearway fire	
Hargincourt	2/17	Situation same as previous day	
Hargincourt	3/17	The enemy shelled our forward Lewis gun intermittently & patrols observed	
Hargincourt	4/17	One forward gun was withdrawn from the front line to the FLESQUIERES area the enemy having broken through the support line	
Hargincourt	5/17	Lewis Gun removed covered fire the morning but two of the outpost guns retired with the enemy	
Hargincourt	6/17	Enemy attacked FLESQUIERES. Lewis gun teams withdrew to Dumont line in guns thought one Lewis gun was lost	
Hargincourt	7/17	The company remained covering the front in support in dug outs. The enemy did not attack during the day	
Hargincourt	8/17	Company was relieved by 175 Machine Gun Company	

WAR DIARY
or
INTELLIGENCE SUMMARY

Army Form C. 2118.

Place	Date	Hour	Summary of Events and Information	Remarks and references to Appendices
Trescault	1/12/17		Company arrived at TRESCAULT 6 a.m.	
Trescault	2/12/17		Company occupied in clearing up & preparing	
Trescault	3/12/17		Camp fatigue. two guns to aircraft work	
Trescault	4/12/17		Camp fatigue. three guns on Anti-aircraft work	
Trescault	5/12/17		Camp fatigue. two guns on Anti-aircraft work	
Trescault	6/12/17		Camp fatigue. three guns on Anti-aircraft work	
Trescault	7/12/17		Camp fatigue. three guns on Anti-aircraft work	
Trescault	8/12/17		Camp fatigue. three guns on Anti-aircraft work	
Trescault	9/12/17		Company relieved 175 Infy in line & 75 SQUIERS with 11 guns & two Anti-aircraft guns at GRAND RAVINE	

WAR DIARY or INTELLIGENCE SUMMARY.

Army Form C. 2118.

original *August* *hint*

Place	Date	Hour	Summary of Events and Information	Remarks and references to Appendices
DEC 1917				
RESQUIERES	16	7.0.0 Rd	Harassing fire. Quiet day.	
RESQUIERES	17	10.0.0 Rd	Harassing fire, otherwise unchanged	
RESQUIERES	18	18.000 Rds	Harassing fire. Enemy artillery fairly active	
RESQUIERES	19	15.000 Rd	Harassing fire. Situation quiet	
RESQUIERES	20	15,500 Rd	Harassing fire. Trench clear about dug-out positions	
RESQUIERES	21	6000 Rd	Harassing fire. Company relieved by 52md Coy. Marched to BERTINCOURT	
BERTINCOURT	22	64 BERTINCOURT	Bn marched to ROCQUIGNY	
ROCQUIGNY	23		Bn cleaning up & marched to BAPAUME entraining at BAPAUME at 2pm. Arrived TINQUES before dark & marched to LIGNERUIL. Arrived about 7pm	Ref. Sgt Sumner
LIGNERUIL	24		General Holiday	

WAR DIARY
INTELLIGENCE SUMMARY

Army Form C. 2118.

Place	Date	Hour	Summary of Events and Information	Remarks and references to Appendices
LONGUEVIL	1/5/17		Company held sports with Horse show & Company	
LONGUEVIL	2/5/17		Lorry at LONGUEVIL for Holiday	
LONGUEVIL	2/5/17		Company training but with equal good	
LONGUEVIL	3/5/17		Holiday	
LONGUEVIL	3/5/17		General training work. Programme carried out by Company	

177 M.G. Coy.

Original

177 MG Coy

Army Form C. 2118

WAR DIARY
or
INTELLIGENCE SUMMARY.
(Erase heading not required.)

177 M.G. Coy

Month of January 1918 Vol. 12

Place	Date	Hour	Summary of Events and Information	Remarks and references to Appendices
Epinoy	1/1/18		Serial training programme of work carried out. Tactical scheme for officers under 2nd in Command	Map ref. I.21.b-7.0 Sheet 51c 20/F
—	2/1/18		Serial training programme of work carried out	10/F
—	3/1/18		Serial training programme of work carried out. Lectures carried out for officers under Brigadier 177 Inf Bde	10/F
—	4/1/18		Serial training programme of work carried out	10/F
—	5/1/18		Serial training programme of work carried out. Lectures carried out for officers under 2nd in Command	15/F
—	6/1/18		Serial training programme of work carried out	15/F
—	7/1/18		Serial training programme of work carried out	20/F
—	8/1/18		Serial training programme of work carried out	15/F
—	9/1/18		Coy inspected by OC	10/F
—	10/1/18		Baths	10/F
—	11/1/18		Inspection by OC in SSC	10/F
—	12/1/18		General training	10/F

WAR DIARY or **INTELLIGENCE SUMMARY**

Army Form C. 2118.

Place	Date	Hour	Summary of Events and Information	Remarks and references to Appendices
HENEREUIL	13/7/18		Church Parade	
	14/7/18	9-10	Company Drill	10/7
		10-11	Rifle Exercises - Spare parts	10/7
	15/7/18	2.30	Divisional Football match	
	16/7/18		General Training Programme of work carried out	10/7
	17/7/18		General Training Programme of work carried out	10/7
	18/7/18		Bath	10/7
	19/7/18		General Training Programme of work carried out	10/7
	20/7/18		Brigade Long distance Run	10/7
	21/7/18		Church Parade	10/7
	22/7/18		General Training Programme of work carried out	10/7
	23/7/18		General Training Programme of work carried out	10/7
	24/7/18		General Training Programme of work carried out	10/7
			Tactical exercise for officers under Brigadier summers	10/7

Original

WAR DIARY
or
INTELLIGENCE SUMMARY

Army Form C. 2118.

Secret

(Erase heading not required.)

Instructions regarding War Diaries and Intelligence Summaries are contained in F.S. Regs., Part II. and the Staff Manual respectively. Title pages will be prepared in manuscript.

Place	Date	Hour	Summary of Events and Information	Remarks and references to Appendices
LIGNEREUIL	24/5/18		Company firing on range at 100 yds & 450 yds Rapid & application practices	10/7
	25/5/18		do	10/7
	26/5/18		G.O.C's inspection (Brig Gen Jones) at 9.30 am of Company & transport on field off LIGNEREUIL-DENIER Rd. Full marching order.	10/7
	27/5/18		11 am Company bathed. Church parade C.E. 11 am. (NON CONFORMISTS 9 am)	10/7
	28/5/18		General training work as per programme	10/7
	29/5/18		General training work as per programme	10/7
	30/5/18		General training work as per programme	10/7
			Ordinary parties & fatigues of stores moved to PENIN G Lab men from 75 Division.	
	31/5/18		Move from LIGNEREUIL to PENIN. West ref of Coy HQ C.22.d.05 (Sheet 51c)	10/7

O.C. No. 177 M.G. Coy
A. Graham Capt.

A6945 Wt. W14422/M160 335,000 12/16 D.D. & L. Forms/C/2118/14.

Army Form C. 2118.

Secret
177 M.G. Coy

Original

WAR DIARY
or
INTELLIGENCE SUMMARY.
(Erase heading not required.)

Vol 13

Place	Date	Hour	Summary of Events and Information	Remarks and references to Appendices
PENIN	1/9/18		Programme – 9 – 10 a.m. P.T.	Map Reference C.22.d.O.5 (Sheet 51C)
			10 – 11.30 a.m. Drill with limbers	
	2/9/18		11.45 – 12.45 Gas instruction & drill	10 f. f.
	3/9/18		2.30 – 3.30 p.m. Cleaning guns & limbers	10 f. f.
			Men requiring inoculation done (about 100).	
	4/9/18		Sunday No parades	
	5/9/18		Guns cleaned & spare parts checked Equipment fitted & cleaned for inspection	10 f. f.
			Inspection of Coys by VI Corps Commander at AMBRINES at 10.30 a.m. Followed by short route march.	10 f. f.
	6/9/18		Morning – Baths at Ambrines	1 f. f.
			Afternoon – Muster Parade	
	7/9/18		Morning – Company training	
			Afternoon – Recreational training	8 f. s.
	8/9/18		Preparing to move.	
	9/9/18		The Company moved to Bouay in Artois	
			Moved to Menchicourt	

O.C. No. 177 M.G. Coy.

August

WAR DIARY
or
INTELLIGENCE SUMMARY
(Erase heading not required.)

Army Form C. 2118.

Place	Date	Hour	Summary of Events and Information	Remarks and references to Appendices
Daours	1/8/18		Moved to MOYENNEVILLE	
	12/8/18		Moved to ERVILLERS	
	13/8/18		Relieved 14 M.G. Coy in the line	
	14/8/18		The whole 16 guns in the line. Situation quiet	
	15/8/18		Enemy Artillery fairly active on our front. Our guns fired harassing fire on various targets.	
	16/8/18		Situation unchanged. Considerable aerial activity. Our enemy machines brought down on our front. Enemy Artillery shelled our batteries but without any damage to our guns. Guns fired 19,17 R.ds. harassing fire on Enemy roads & tracks.	
	17/8/18		Considerable aerial activity + enemy counter battery work at night. The enemy bombed our back areas considerably.	
	18/8/18		Enemy Aircraft fairly active over our lines. Otherwise the day was quiet.	

A.O.O. No. 177 M.G. Corps

WAR DIARY
or
INTELLIGENCE SUMMARY.

Army Form C. 2118.

(Erase heading not required.)

Place	Date	Hour	Summary of Events and Information	Remarks and references to Appendices
Trenches	1/4/18		Senior shelled very heavily throughout the day our sniping guns engaged some enemy working parties	JC
"	2/4/18		The day was quiet our guns fired 8350 Rds harassing fire in conjunction with the artillery	JC
"	3/4/18		Enemy artillery active at intervals during the day our guns reported on parties sniped artillery active in retaliation during the day A.M.	JC
"	4/4/18		Went up to our right 3. Team all quiet 4.0. Enemy shelled Bulloceny during the day sniping guns disposed some enemy parties allowance quiet	JC
"	5/4/18		The day was quiet our artillery was very active between 7 P.M.- 9 P.M. our guns fired 3970 Rds on SS4 on the left	JC
	6/4/18		Found enemy artillery very active brought down enemy by our A.A. Guns	JC

O.C. No. 177 M.G. Coy

Army Form C. 2118.

WAR DIARY
or
INTELLIGENCE SUMMARY.
(Erase heading not required.)

Original
Leave.

Place	Date	Hour	Summary of Events and Information	Remarks and references to Appendices
In field	27/4/18		Situation normal the week relieved by 2nd M.G.Coy.	OS
	28/4/18		Coy in Reserve at _____ many enemy planes	OS
			Guns & checking defensive O.P.	
			[signature] Capt.	
			O.C. No. 177 M.G. Coy.	

www.ingramcontent.com/pod-product-compliance
Lightning Source LLC
Chambersburg PA
CBHW081423160426
43193CB00013B/2181